ARMSTRONG SIDDELEY

ARMSTRONG SIDDELEY

THE SPHINX WITH THE HEART OF A LION

Bruce Lindsay
Foreword by Simon Pearce

© Bruce Lindsay 2010

First edition May, 2010

ISBN 978-0-646-52723-9

No part of the text of this book may be reproduced in any form or by any means without
the prior written permission of the author, which will not be unreasonably withheld.

Author's contacts: 2 Hawthorn Road, Stirling 5152, South Australia

Email: blindsay@chariot.net.au

Published by the Lindsay Family Trust, Chalong, Phuket 83100, Thailand

Book design and layout by

Mark Thomas, Graphic Alliance Pty Ltd, 6/198 Greenhill Road, Eastwood 5063, South Australia

Printed by Everbest Printing Co Ltd, China

Print run of 1000 copies

DEDICATION

John Bull 15.02.1937 – 20.10.1996

v

Courtesy Messenger Guardian. Published April 23, 1996

DEDICATION

John Bull 15.02.1937 – 20.10.1996

13/11/76

John Bull

Courtesy Messenger Guardian. Published April 23, 1996

SYD · 000

John Bull
76

John Bull

About John Bull

R ambunctious is the single word that best describes John Bull. His enthusiasm for his passions was all-pervading and infectious.

John was born the eldest of three boys, and upon the departure of their father he sought employment sooner than he might otherwise have done, in order to support his mother and siblings. Beginning as a cadet designer with Chrysler Australia, he suffered damage to his eyes, and joined the Post Office to work at night and preserve his vision. By choice he performed menial work with the Office for the rest of his working life, leaving him the mental space to pursue his love of art and motoring.

He always admired the physical beauty of British coachwork, especially when attached to Armstrong Siddeley, Daimler, Rolls-Royce and Bentley cars. With patience and persistence he developed a distinctively detailed drawing style, and illustrated handsome motor-cars both for his own amusement and on commissions from their owners.

Many of his drawings were published in Martin Bennett's 1976 book *Rolls-Royce and Bentley The History of The Car*. Public display of his works included a one-man exhibition at Adelaide's Lombard Galleries in 1982, and in 1983 he collaborated with celebrated Adelaide cartoonist, Ross Bateup, to illustrate a collection of whimsical images celebrating the Silver Jubilee of the South Australian Rolls-Royce Owners Club.

His was a cerebral and academic interest, which led him to carefully collect and catalogue a large archive of original material. Happily that archive survives in the care of the Armstrong Siddeley Car Club and the Rolls-Royce Owners Club in South Australia.

John was ever the social being, loved a laugh, loved a drink, and frequently signed off his voluminous letters with drawings of frothing beer steins or overflowing wine glasses. He rejoiced in the fine old stone buildings sprinkled around Adelaide, and combined patronage of the region's many historic pubs with fine drawings of them – almost invariably with one of his Armstrong Siddeleys parked outside.

He was a founding member of the South Australian branch of the Armstrong Siddeley Car Club, and while he owned various models of the marque throughout his life, his favourite was the 18hp Hurricane drophead coupé retained until his death.

In tribute to John's unselfish life, in which he suppressed his own disappointments while enriching the lives of others, we reproduce just a few of his distinctive artworks involving Armstrong Siddeley cars drawn from the city he loved.

Remains of the Cornwell Inn, Willunga. Licensed 1853-1876

John Bull
1972

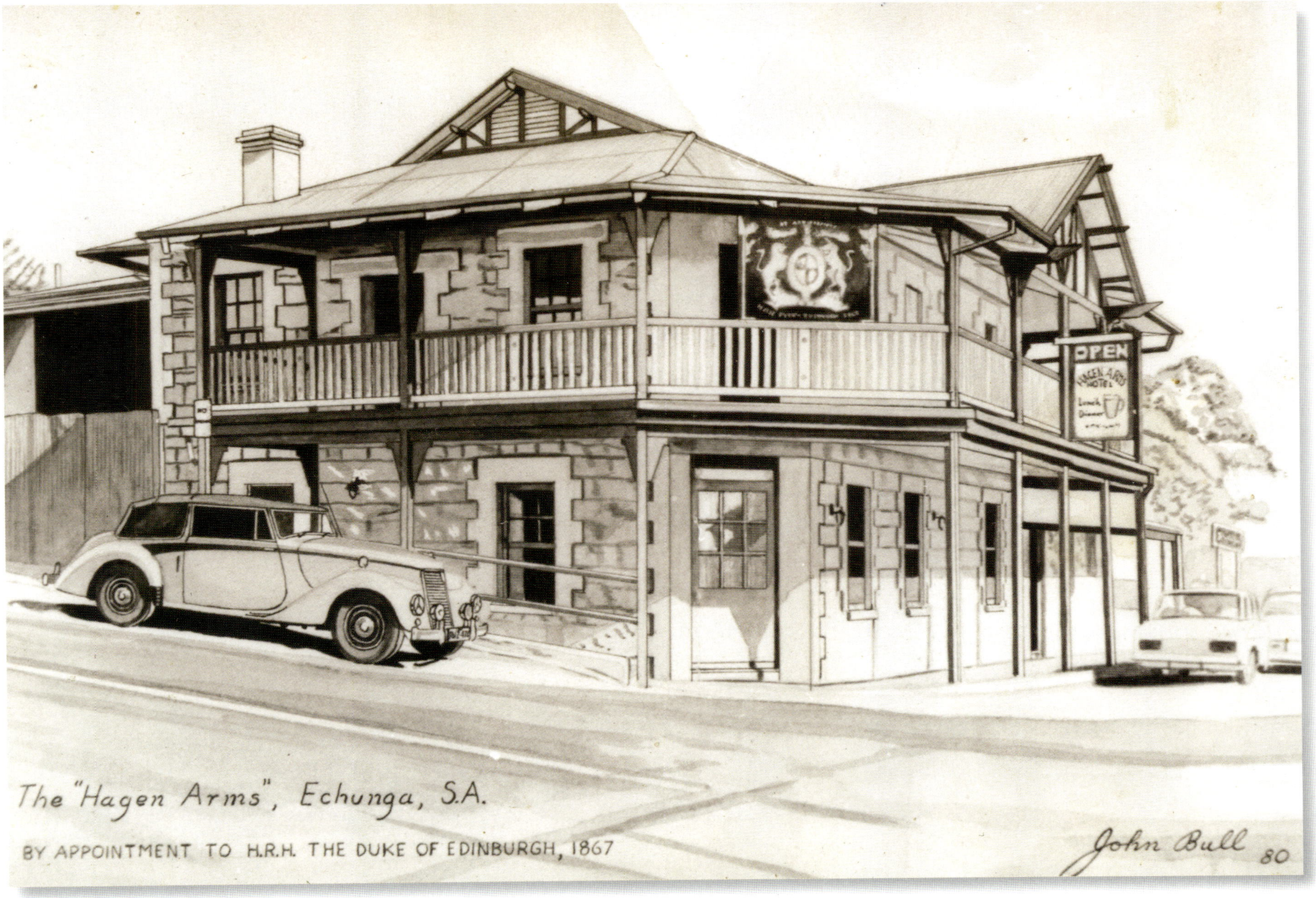

The "Hagen Arms", Echunga, S.A.

BY APPOINTMENT TO H.R.H. THE DUKE OF EDINBURGH, 1867

John Bull 80

John Bull

CONTENTS

FOREWORD *by Simon Pearce*

Some months ago on hearing through the grapevine that someone by the name of Bruce Lindsay was writing a book on Armstrong Siddeleys, I remember being rather surprised. There had been a number of books published over the last few years and I wondered how the subject would be approached this time.

I then heard that Bruce, who lives in Australia, would welcome help with his project. On coming into contact with him and seeing his superb recently published book "Lancia – 70 Years of Trailblazing", I was immediately impressed, not only by the quality of the book, but by Bruce's obvious enthusiasm and refreshing approach utilising contemporary photographs and brochures and the inclusion of a DVD containing many more evocative images. I was hooked! In due course I and others were helping in various ways.

As well as being a Lancia aficionado Bruce has been an enthusiastic Armstrong Siddeley owner, but would be the first to admit that his knowledge is not fully comprehensive. I was struck by his extraordinary energy and quest for accuracy.

Armstrong Siddeley cars are often considered to be staid but this reputation is seldom deserved. When readers see the illustrations of pre-war cars in this book many will be surprised by the huge variety of bodies that were fitted not only in-house but by others, including many of the most prestigious coachbuilders of the day. The pioneering use of light alloys, preselector gearboxes and variable power steering all show the company's use of cutting edge technology. Even immediately after the war when model ranges were much reduced by virtually all manufacturers, Armstrong Siddeley offered a choice of transmissions and later they were probably the only car maker to list three gearbox options on one model!

This engaging new book is not only for the dyed-in-the-wool Armstrong Siddeley fanatic – it will appeal to all those who have an interest in motorcars in that fascinating period between the Great War and 1960. I feel privileged to have made a small contribution to this work.

Simon Pearce

December 2009

About Simon Pearce

B orn just before the introduction of the post-war Armstrong Siddeley cars Simon has spent most of his life in Walton-on-the-Hill and Banstead in Surrey. He has been semi-retired for a number of years from a career, mainly as a working director of various companies, exporting motor transport spares and engineering commodities.

He is married and has a son and a daughter.

Contrary to what some motoring colleagues might think, Simon did not start life with a silver sphinx in his mouth, but first became interested in Armstrong Siddeleys whilst still at school, when his father bought a 1936 20/25hp. This was fifteen years after the war, when families with a car thought themselves fortunate. Simon revelled in this large car which he drove both before and after taking his driving test which he passed within a few days of his seventeenth birthday. He was to own, amongst other cars, a number of pre-war Armstrong Siddeleys. When Jackie married Simon he came with a Siddeley Special and it is this same car that they enjoy today along with their Stoneleigh Chummy.

Simon is interested in motors and motoring up to the 1960s and has been a member of the Armstrong Siddeley Owners' Club for nearly fifty years, during which time he has undertaken various roles including that of director and registrar. He is a trustee of the Armstrong Siddeley Heritage Trust and a member of the Rolls-Royce Heritage Trust (whose Coventry branch cover the aero and car products of Parkside). He is also a member of The Society of Automotive Historians in Britain and the Surrey Vintage Vehicle Society.

ACKNOWLEDGEMENTS

While the author's name may get star billing on its cover, any book that attempts to accurately render the history of a motoring marque depends on the material supplied by its many contributors.

South Australian Armstrong Siddeley enthusiast, Andrew Christophersen, viewed my illustrated history of the Lancia marque (*Lancia – 70 Years of Trailblazing*) and mused on the possibility of producing another covering Siddeleys in similar fashion.

Like the Lancia title, this book strips away latter-day impressions of motor-cars which may be badly worn or modified from the original, by employing only images, driving impressions, media comments and illustrated advertisements published when the cars were new. It could only happen with the ready assistance of many enthusiasts worldwide, who have kindly provided the raw material now published.

Original sales catalogues are used for most of the book's illustrations, and I am deeply indebted to collectors Chris Allen, Selwyn Allen, Robert Penn Bradly, Frank Cooke, Andrew Christophersen, Wayne Lander and Simon Pearce for their generous loan or scans of rare publications; I am particularly grateful to Peter Hills and Helen Andrews for facilitating my access to Peter's wonderful collection.

Supply of some evocative and hitherto unpublished period photographs also help to establish the authentic period feel, for which I acknowledge David and Yvonne Armstrong, Robert Penn Bradly, Rowan Fitzpatricke, Bryan Goodman and the John Bull Collection. Items reproduced from Penn's long-time collection were sourced from Armstrong Siddeley Motors Ltd, Rolls-Royce Industrial and Marine Gas Turbine Division, and the Buckle Motors (Sydney, New South Wales, Australia) historical collection. Bryan Goodman's remarkable photograph collection has yielded some gems for which I am particularly grateful, and to Keith Harding for supplying high-resolution scans. Those from the John Bull Collection came courtesy of the South Australian Branch of the Armstrong Siddeley Car Club.

Original illustrated advertisements contribute to the flavour, and for supply of originals I thank Frank Ashton and Steve Thompson.

Angela Verschoor generously collated a representative sample of Armstrong Siddeley promotional material from 1919-1960, displayed on the DVD attached to the inside back cover of the book, which will itself become an invaluable information resource for owners, enthusiasts and collectors.

For advice on the correctness of data, proof-reading and suggestions for improvement, I am deeply grateful to Chris Allen, Selwyn Allen, Andrew Christophersen, Frank Cooke and Simon Pearce, all of whom have ground their way through drafts to help produce the finished product.

To my Editor and friend Max Anderson I express my thanks for his peerless and patient work, and to Mark Thomas of Graphic Alliance Pty Ltd for the application of his outstanding talents to the book's design and layout. Everbest Printing Co and their Australian Manager, Lionel Marz, have produced printing and binding of which any author would be proud, for which I sincerely thank them.

Please accept that credit for the production of this book rests with many folk beyond the author, and I hope I will be forgiven if I have unwittingly omitted any contributor – however minor – from the list of acknowledgements.

We all hope that you enjoy the read.
Bruce Lindsay, Adelaide, December 2009

INTRODUCTION

The essence of the Armstrong Siddeley marque is difficult to define. John Davenport Siddeley was an entrepreneur well-versed in marketing, rather than an engineering idealist treading his own path. The motor-cars produced under his watch reflected his astute market sense, and were not confined to those of a single genre. Identifying market niches in the inter-war years, he supervised the production of models as pedestrian as the Stoneleigh light car and as patrician as the Siddeley Special. He sold cars popular with elderly vicars and entered others in major rallies and trials.

Writing in *The Motor* of January 5, 1955 following the release of the Armstrong Siddeley Sapphire, Philip A Turner came close to encapsulating the company's design and marketing ethos when he wrote: "Armstrong Siddeley cars have always occupied an unusual position in the world of motoring, probably because the philosophy behind their production has for so long differed from the line of thought of most other manufacturers. Right from the very early days of motoring it was the paramount aim of their creator, John Siddeley, the first Baron Kenilworth, to produce a car which was the natural successor to the gentleman's carriage-and-pair in which 'carriage folk' could travel with dignity and in comfort. Even in 1904 the Siddeley cars which were the ancestors of the present models were being advertised as 'durable, quiet and economical' while the pre-Kaiser War Siddeley-Deaseys (sic), with their coffin-shaped bonnets foreshadowing the present Armstrong Siddeley radiator, were described on the front

covers of copies of *The Motor* of that period as 'comfortable carriages'. In brief, Siddeley-inspired cars have always been comfortable means of travel rather than pieces of engineering to which bodies were added somewhat as an afterthought.

"Not that the cars have been lacking in technical excellence; the Siddeley-Deaseys were among the earliest cars to be fitted with self-starters, had dry-sump lubrication and used much light alloy in their construction. The first Armstrong Siddeley, the massive 1919 Thirty, owed much to the experience gained by the company in the manufacture of Siddeley Puma aircraft engines which were produced at the rate of 700 a month during the first world war. In 1928 the company pioneered the use of the preselector gearbox and in 1933 the fabulous Siddeley Special with its Hiduminium light-alloy engine was placed in production. Nevertheless, the Armstrong Siddeley had come to be regarded as a highly respectable and rather sober carriage, inhabited exclusively by the best country families and the directors of banks".

This image was strengthened by early patronage of the marque by Royalty in Britain and abroad, by Prime Ministers, by high-profile public figures including speed ace Sir Malcolm Campbell, and airmen Sir John Cobham and Sir Charles Kingsford-Smith. Siddeley was always happy to associate his cars with aircraft, with which there was public fascination particularly in the '20s and '30s. Advertisements and sales material from 1921 frequently contained images of aircraft, mention of aircraft, and latterly the adoption of aircraft names. Australian distributor Clemenger Motors of Melbourne used aircraft engine names Lynx, Panther and Jaguar to promote pre-war models, while after 1945 the company's Hurricane, Lancaster, Typhoon, Tempest and Whitley model names were reminders of the success of Armstrong Siddeley-powered aircraft in World War 2. The Sapphire was named after the company's successful jet engine.

Consistent throughout the model range was a refusal to compromise build quality or passenger comfort, underlining Philip Turner's characterisation of the breed as 'comfortable carriages'. The first of many marketing slogans – adopted for the Thirty and the early Eighteen – was 'Motor Carriages of Perfect Comfort'. This was supported by the coachwork's emphasis on interior fittings, especially for the closed cars, which transported occupants to their destination in surroundings not dissimilar to drawing rooms or club lounges. The Deasy company under Siddeley's direction had acquired the Burlington Carriage Company in August, 1913, ensuring that the design and build quality of coachwork attached to the chassis of Deasy and later Armstrong Siddeley cars could be controlled to the companies' satisfaction.

The dictum for chauffeurs was that the master/mistress should be unaware when the accelerator or the brake was being applied, so blistering acceleration was never a priority. Yet even the least powerful Armstrong Siddeley – the Twelve – matched its contemporaries for top speed, and toured faster than most. Some of the larger-engined models – the New Twenty, the 25hp and the Special – combined armchair comfort with performance often compared by motoring journalists to 'sportscars'.

Siddeley realised that a whole new market existed for cars which required minimal physical effort to drive, and introduced the 'self-change' preselector transmission to attract novices and especially female drivers. Yet the Wilson transmission also drove the all-conquering ERA racing cars and many of the highly competitive 'thirties sports cars such as Riley, MG and Squire.

The early inclusion of one-shot chassis lubrication, permanently fitted jacks and – in some models – vanity cases and flower vases were openly intended to convince women that motoring was not the exclusive province of men.

The more adventurous coachwork of the 1930s broadened the marque's appeal with more sporting lines and lively colour schemes, but always emphasising comfort and durability. Following World War 2 the company acknowledged that the Sixteen needed more power, and responded with an increase in engine capacity, while continuing to produce elegant and commodious means of transporting passengers.

The 3.4-litre Sapphire and its 4-litre Star Sapphire successor embodied the very best of the previous decades of production, being elegant, comfortable and swift motor-cars. They were probably further ahead of their competitors than most potential buyers realised.

THE ARMSTRONG SIDDELEY HERITAGE TRUST

This book offers contemporary images, company pronouncements and assessments of the cars when new. It will hopefully allow many motoring enthusiasts to view the company and its products through new eyes, reaching their own conclusions on the place in the history of motoring deserved by this under-appreciated marque, rather than subscribing to the bias of some commentators.

NOTES ON DATA PANELS:

Since Armstrong Siddeley constantly developed every model, readers should use the data panels for general comparative purposes only, as they cannot hope to be comprehensive. Panels attempt to show correct data for the model as introduced, and include variations where known and confirmed. Production figures are subject to variation according to source, and must be taken as approximate only.

Bruce Lindsay, Adelaide, December, 2009

The Armstrong Siddeley Heritage Trust is a United Kingdom based charity set up in 2005, to ensure that future generations have the opportunity to fully appreciate the significant role that J.D.Siddeley and Armstrong Siddeley played in the world's motor and other industries. It is primarily involved in providing the means and organisation to safeguard the names, records and products of the various companies for posterity.

This involves the collation of all information currently existing or known of, and the Trust is always keen to hear about any records or original memorabilia in your possession or of which you may be aware.

Friends of the Trust receive regular news on progress and the latest achievements of the Trust.

Should you wish to become a Friend, make a one-off gift, leave a legacy to the Trust or just make general enquiries, please contact:

Mr Bill Brenchley
Kingston Springs Farm
Brownstone Road
Kingswear
Devon
England
TQ6 0EG

By Land — By Air — By Armstrong Siddeley

ARMSTRONG SIDDELEY

CHAPTER 2

THE FIRST ARMSTRONG SIDDELEY
THE 30HP – 1920-1932

John Siddeley observed that industrial development and automotive technology in America had been largely unaffected by the war which crippled development in Europe. He quietly imported a Marmon Model 34 motor car in 1918 for detailed inspection, selecting this model for its unconventional design and advanced use of aluminium alloy, with consequent good ratio of weight to engine power.

After the establishment of Armstrong Siddeley Motors Limited in October, 1919, first deliveries of the car design on which Siddeley had been engaged were made in April, 1920. Its form may have been influenced by US contemporaries, but its execution was quintessentially British. Its massive architecture and therefore its intended market reflected the wealth generated by industrialists during the war, and the public clamouring for mobility in motor cars ranging from the basic cycle-car to the most opulent limousine. Referring to the first car's square-rigged shape and imposing height, Mr Inglis – the then-manager of the company's in-house Burlington Carriage Works – declared "The top hat is always smarter than the bowler".

The Thirty was built on a steel chassis of mammoth side-members which at some points exceeded 12" in depth, a wheelbase of 11'3", a track of 4'8" and an overall length of 16'4½". While there were gaitered semi-elliptic springs at the front, cantilevers were employed at the rear, adjustable for height according to the weight of coachwork. Lever-arm shock-absorbers were fitted, initially only at the rear. Initially there were rear-wheel brakes only, where side-by-side shoes in huge drums were operated by rods; front wheel brakes on the Perrot system were later offered as extra-cost options, following the pattern used on Delage and later Bentley cars. Steering was by worm and wheel mechanism and wheels were solid steel discs secured by eight studs. Running-boards were permanently affixed to the side-members, thereby reinforcing the frame, as on the Marmon car studied by Siddeley.

To this chassis was mated a 4960cc six-cylinder engine, built on an alloy crankcase with two cast iron blocks of three cylinders, surmounted by separate cylinder heads incorporating overhead valves. Pushrods were carried in separate external alloy tubes, there was magneto ignition and electric start. With bores of 88.9mm and stroke of 133.4mm the engine was RAC rated at 29.5hp, and there were three bearings each for the crankshaft and the camshaft. Unusually for a new design of the time, cooling continued the Siddeley-Deasy's vaned flywheel, drawing air through the huge vee-shaped patented radiator and controlling the airflow with undertrays essential to the efficiency of the system. Fuel was fed by gravity from a scuttle-mounted fuel tank initially to a dual Claudel Hobson carburettor with twin stranglers; a float-controlled fuel gauge was mounted on the scuttle.

While the three-speed crash gearbox was conventional, its mounting was novel. A short and stout jack-shaft transmitted drive to the 'box itself, which was mounted on a cross-member and attached at its rear to the front of the torque tube, through which the tailshaft drove the rear axle. The very heavy flywheel and low engine compression meant that gearchanges were necessarily leisurely and the expertise needed for quiet changes considerable. Fortunately for the unskilled driver the massive torque of the engine allowed travel from 5mph to an effective maximum of about 65mph on top gear.

Following the policy established by the Deasy company, Armstrong Siddeley developed the capacity of its own coachbuilder – the Burlington Carriage Company – to produce a variety of standard body designs, over which the company exercised quality control and advertised prices for complete cars. The works were however happy to accommodate buyers' special requirements – especially but not only those of British royalty – so many cars departed from the standard specification. These and all subsequent Armstrong Siddeley cars were subjected to a policy of continuous improvement and modification, regardless of the application of particular series numbers.

The factory built almost all components for their first motorcar, including rear axle, brakes, front suspension, steering and clutch. Contemporary reports from Armstrong Siddeley executives tell: "That car certainly was a winner for sales...we could not make them fast enough".

After completion of about 2317 cars in April, 1925, a second series of 30hp cars was introduced. Its principal difference was the change to a one-piece cylinder block, even though there remained two separate cylinder heads. The pushrods were enclosed within the engine block,

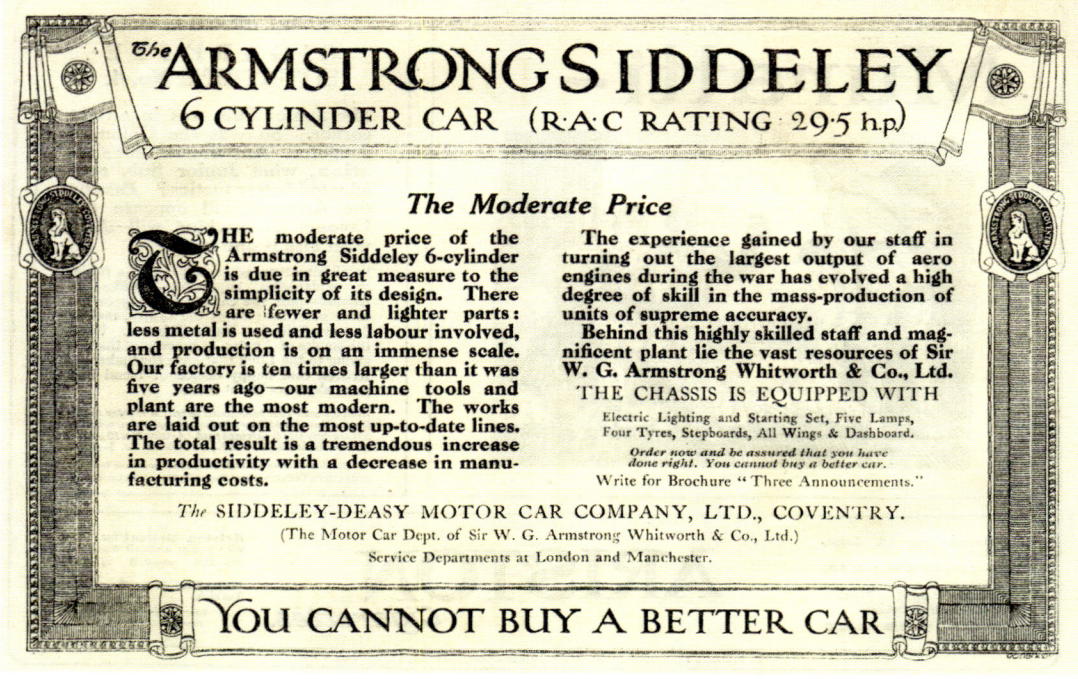

The ARMSTRONG SIDDELEY

6 CYLINDER CAR (R·A·C RATING 29·5 h.p)

The Moderate Price

THE moderate price of the Armstrong Siddeley 6-cylinder is due in great measure to the simplicity of its design. There are fewer and lighter parts: less metal is used and less labour involved, and production is on an immense scale. Our factory is ten times larger than it was five years ago—our machine tools and plant are the most modern. The works are laid out on the most up-to-date lines. The total result is a tremendous increase in productivity with a decrease in manufacturing costs.

The experience gained by our staff in turning out the largest output of aero engines during the war has evolved a high degree of skill in the mass-production of units of supreme accuracy.

Behind this highly skilled staff and magnificent plant lie the vast resources of Sir W. G. Armstrong Whitworth & Co., Ltd.

THE CHASSIS IS EQUIPPED WITH

Electric Lighting and Starting Set, Five Lamps, Four Tyres, Stepboards, All Wings & Dashboard.

Order now and be assured that you have done right. You cannot buy a better car.

Write for Brochure "Three Announcements."

The SIDDELEY-DEASY MOTOR CAR COMPANY, LTD., COVENTRY.

(The Motor Car Dept. of Sir W. G. Armstrong Whitworth & Co., Ltd.)

Service Departments at London and Manchester.

YOU CANNOT BUY A BETTER CAR

gearbox ratios remained the same, but four-wheel brakes became standard fare.

From January, 1928, came a third series, powered by a genuine monobloc version of the same engine, with one-piece cylinder head. A new chassis with 11'4½" wheelbase was upswept at the rear, where the fuel tank and luggage grid sat between the rails. From October, 1928 the newly-introduced Wilson preselector gearbox was available for an extra £50, as was a Daimler-sourced fluid flywheel from 1930, while the Vee radiator was higher and narrower to accommodate the body styles then in vogue.

The last of the 30hp cars were fitted Luvax shock-absorbers all round, dashboard instruments were revised and the battery

was relocated inside the frame. The model was still catalogued as an enclosed limousine or landaulette for £1250 in 1933, and at least one of them was powered by the new engine destined for the Siddeley Special.

With a total production of more than 2700, the first Armstrong Siddeley car must be termed a commercial success, even though its production spanned 10-12 years. The Thirty was rightly regarded as a vehicle of high quality, but through canny manufacturing processes its price was considerably lower than its competitors – mainly Daimler, Napier and Rolls-Royce. Prince Albert – later to become King George VI – was an early and loyal customer who commissioned various cars both on the 30hp and the later 18hp chassis, despite the fact that his first personal car was a 16hp Austin.

The 'Siddeley Six' laid a firm foundation on which forty years of motor manufacturing was built. Owners' opinions published in contemporary sales material included; "My Armstrong Siddeley 30hp has now done 132,000 miles which I think must be nearly a record for a car going to be six years old in April (*1927*), and the best part is that it is going strong to-day, nearly as good as ever"; "This car (*a 30hp*) has travelled well over 96,000 miles. It has never yet been held up on the road for other than tyre trouble. On other than short runs the consumption can be taken at 18 miles to the gallon. My chauffeur informs me that the consumption of engine oil is negligible"; and "This 30hp car was purchased by the Education Authority in January, 1921, and was continually in use until March, 1926. My chauffeur informs me that the car did at least 165,000 miles during that period. The car was used throughout the whole of the County of Lanark in many of the outlying districts of which it experienced severe tests with the hilly and rough conditions of the road".

A charming tale, which is thought to relate to a Thirty, was published in Glasgow's *The Western Leader* newspaper in October, 1932, and recounted in *The Evening and the Morning*, headed 'A Fifty Shilling Motor'; "Two Hillhead men and a 50 shilling automobile figured in a wonderful motoring feat last week. The two men were Norman Goudei and James Dornan, who carry on business in Otago Lane, Hillhead, as motor engineers. They specialise in buying old models for breaking up.

"For business purposes it became necessary for them to make a trip to London, but to their dismay they found that all their hiring cars were out, and the only one they had in the garage was a 1924 model Armstrong Siddeley, which they had bought for 50 shillings (then £2.10.0 or $5), and which had been put on the 'shelf' to be broken up as scrap. They finally decided to make the journey with this car, and set off for London in it, the car being in practically the same condition as when they had bought it. Much to their surprise, the car successfully completed the double journey, giving a performance which they would have believed impossible. Their route lay through Liverpool, and the journey took twenty-four hours, twelve hours each way.

"Not a single car passed this 'scrap' model on the road. On the contrary, it passed everything it saw in front of it as occasion demanded, and drew away from all cars that came up with it, including 1932 sports models capable of exceptional speed. For hours on end the two engineers, who drove alternately, were able to keep the throttle wide open, a feat they believe would be impossible with any car produced today for under £500.

"Every moment they expected to see the engine fly to pieces, but nothing of the sort happened, the only trouble they experienced being a puncture on the return journey in one of the tyres bought with the car.

"The 'scrap' model is now back in Glasgow, and the owners have decided that, for the present, it would be a sin to break up such an amazing bus. It is still running splendidly, none the worse for its long journey of nine hundred miles, which was completed with only one day's stay in London".

Motor Carriages of Perfect Comfort!

THE new Armstrong-Siddeley 6-cylinder Car is of entirely original design, and embodies the experience gained during the past four years in the production of aircraft engines aggregating over 2,000,000 (two million) horse-power.

You cannot buy a better car.

It is a motor-carriage of high efficiency, stately appearance and ample power—constructed of the best materials.

It is light. It is comfortable. It is dependable. It runs smoothly, silently, and is easily managed. Maintenance costs are small. The low price at which it is sold is due to its simple design and to quantity production.

PRICE of CHASSIS Lucas Engine Starter and Electric Lighting complete with 5 Lamps, 4 Wheels and Spare Rim, EQUIPPED WITH 4 Tyres, Stepboards, all Wings and Dashboard. **£720**

Saloon Double Phaeton (as illustrated) - - - - £1000.

ARMSTRONG - SIDDELEY MOTORS LIMITED COVENTRY

(Formerly The Siddeley-Deasy Motor Car Co., Ltd.), Allied with Sir W. G. Armstrong Whitworth & Co., Ltd.

LONDON : 10, Old Bond Street, W. I

Olympia Stand 72.

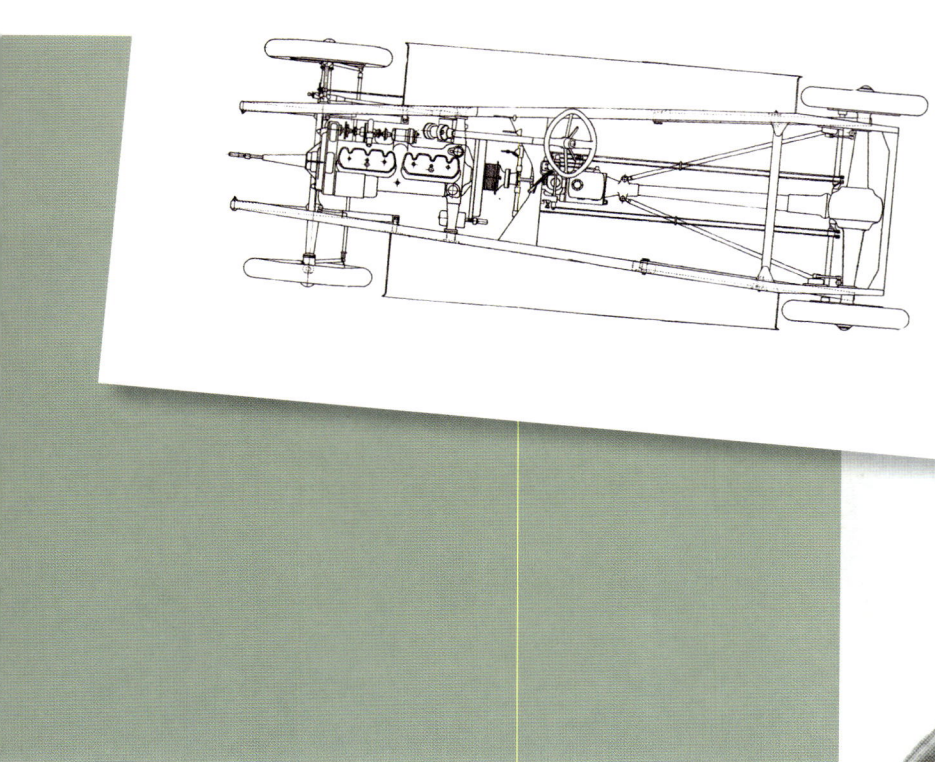

Above: 30hp chassis in plan view. Note the stout triangulated bracing to the rear axle, and the integral running boards strengthening the chassis frame.

Right: 30hp first series chassis with front wings fitted, and showing the disc wheels which typified the model.

Above: Nearside of the first series 30hp engine. Note the updraught Claudel Hobson carburettor with heated inlet, and the two separate cylinder blocks and heads.

Left: Offside of the early engine, with separate external pushrod tubes, and gear drive to the water pump and magneto. Note the high standard of finish and extensive use of aluminium alloy.

Above: Handbook illustration of the first facia. The starter pedal is located on the toeboard.

Above right: Detail of the separate gearbox, mounted on the forward end of the torque tube. This arrangement survived on all Armstrong Siddeley cars until gearboxes were attached to engines in 1937.

Right: Initially only two-wheel brakes were standard on the 30hp.

Far right: Front wheel brakes on the Perrot pattern were offered as extra cost options from 1922.

Above: While Armstrong Siddeley's in-house coachbuilder, the Burlington Carriage Co, supplied most of the bodies for the 30hp, this fine limousine with division was built by Mann Egerton.

Top: Mann Egerton built this imposing enclosed landaulette on the first series 30hp chassis.

Harrods Private Car Hire Servi[ce]

This shows one of our more moderatel[y] priced Cars.

To those who do not wish a Car built to their own special requirements, Harrods can supply one of their standard Cars on exceptionally low terms. Harrods will supply a first class Car equal in appearance and offering equal service to the more expensive variety. The varied range of Cars makes it impossible to give full details in this small booklet, but Harrods will be delighted to send a representative with a Car to drive you to the garage and point out the many fine examples of coachwork on view there. You will find that every possible requirement is catered for. From **£50** a month.

HARRODS LTD   LONDON S[W]

12

Above: Lavish 30hp rear compartment as offered for vehicle hire.

Right: 30hp and 18hp cars were popular with hire companies.

Opposite page: Magnificent barrel-sided open tourer, possibly by Barker, on the early series chassis.

Top left: This less elaborate open tourer was built in the late 1920s by Burlington.

Top centre: Also by Burlington, showing their distinctive front-opening front doors, is this imposing enclosed limousine.

Top right: Burlington enclosed landaulette, thoughtfully covering the driver if not entirely protecting him from the elements.

Right: The 'Sociable' or close-coupled two-door saloon was another popular Burlington style.

Far right: The 'Sociable' design was also available as this open two-door tourer.

Above: The second series 30hp cars, introduced in 1925, typically wore more modern and colourful coachwork, including this Richmond Enclosed Limousine by Burlington.

Right: Impression of the palatial rear compartment of the Richmond limousine.

The Burlington-built Shrewsbury Enclosed Limousine in suitably opulent surroundings.

Above: Burlington's Winchester Enclosed Landaulette.

Left: Detail of the rear compartment of the Winchester Landaulette, showing its removable occasional seats and glass division.

By 1931 the Burlington limousine was looking dated, despite its higher radiator and American-influenced coachwork.

ARMSTRONG
SIDDELEY
SIXES
12 h.p., 15 h.p., 20 h.p., 30 h.p.
for
1930
See
The Successful
Self - Changing
4-Speed Gear
OLYMPIA : STAND 127

You cannot buy
a better Car

Write for Catalogue L.81
ARMSTRONG SIDDELEY MOTORS LIMITED, COVENTRY
LONDON : 10 OLD BOND STREET, W.1
MANCHESTER : 35 KING STREET WEST
Agents in all principal towns

BUY BRITISH AND KEEP YOUR ⬧ COUNTRYMEN EMPLOYED

Above: Brochure illustration from 1933 showing the 30hp enclosed limousine with coachwork by Burlington, offered for £1250.

Right: One attempt to modernise the second series cars was this shapely closed limousine by Norfolk coachbuilder Norvic, dating from 1930.

Factory designation	30hp	30hp Mark 2	
Date introduced	April 1920	April 1925	January 1928
Motor type	vertical 6-cyl 4-stroke water-cooled bi-bloc ohv	monobloc, dual cyl heads	genuine monobloc incl cyl head
Dimensions	89 X 133mm = 4960cc	same	same
Fuel feed	gravity feed to dual choke Claudel Hobson carb	same	rear-mounted tank and vacuum feed
Ignition	BTH magneto	same	same
Transmission type	3-speeds & Rev crash gearbox	optional Wilson 4-speed preselective gearbox + £50	Wilson gearbox standardised (from 1928)
Clutch	multi-disc steel plate with fabric disc		
Steering	worm & wheel	same	worm & segment
Suspension			
Front	semi-elliptic springs, no dampers	Luvax shock absorbers introduced	same
Rear	cantilever springs height adjustable, lever arm dampers	same	
Brakes	rear drums with two parallel sets of shoes	4-wheel brakes standardised	same
	Perrot 4-wheel brakes optional at £35 extra from 1922		
Wheels	32" detachable steel discs	same	same
Tyres	820 X 135mm	same	same
Dimensions			
Wheelbase	11'3"	11'4½"	same
Track front	4'8"	same	same
Track rear	4'8"	same	same
Overall length	15'4"	16'4½"	15'5½"
Overall width	depending on coachwork – Richmond limousine 5'8"		
Height	depending on coachwork – Richmond limo 6'8"		
Unladen weight	40cwt typically		
Factory coachwork	Open Tourer, Double Phaeton Sociable, Sociable Saloon, Limousine, Saloon Double Phaeton, Landaulette, Limousine, Open Drive Landaulette	7-seat tourer, sports tourer, Richmond enclosed limousine, Special enclosed limousine, Enclosed limousine, Enclosed Landaulette, Special enclosed Landaulette, Touring landaulette, Shrewsbury Touring limousine, Canterbury Pullman limousine, Saloon limousine	Enclosed limousine or landaulette
Variants	Coachbuilt cars including Connaught, Hibbard & Darrin, Hooper, Lawton-Goodman, Mann-Egerton and Mulliner across all series		
Performance			
Max speed (mph)	65mph	same	same
Fuel consumption (mpg)	13½		
Number produced	Mark 1: 2317 Mark 2: 257 Mark 3: 151		
Prices	(1920) Chassis £720 Tourer £960 Sociable £980 Saloon £1000 Double phaeton sociable £1020 Landaulette £1140, (1921) Chassis £875 Tourer & Open Sociable £1190 Saloon £1345 Limousine £1400 (1927) Chassis £750 Shrewsbury touring landaulette £1150 Wincester enclosed landaulette £1250 Richmond enclosed limousine £1250 Cheltenham Pullman limousine £1300 (fluid flywheel; £50 extra) (1933) Enclosed limousine or landaulette £1350		
Date last produced	July 1932 (but still catalogued for the 1933 season)		

21

CHAPTER 11

THE 18HP 20HP NEW 20HP 20-25HP AND 25HP

John Siddeley recognised that, however successful his elaborate Thirty, the market was heaving with demand for cars that were smaller and cheaper. The 18hp model released at Olympia in 1921 was his answer.

Effectively this was a Thirty reduced in size but not in quality. Built on a 10' wheelbase, its bi-bloc overhead valve six cylinder engine drove a three-speed crash gearbox attached to the forward end of the torque tube, was sprung by semi-elliptic springs in front and cantilevers at the rear, and used two-wheel brakes. The three-bearing engine displaced 2386cc from bores of 69.5mm and stroke of 104.8mm, but its shorter axle ratio still allowed it to reach 56.18mph. Such performance roughly approximated that of the larger car, for almost half the price.

The Eighteen chassis similarly employed a dual Claudel Hobson carburettor, gravity fuel feed, and integral running boards. Wheels were solid steel discs, and four-wheel brakes were available from 1925 at extra cost.

Like the Thirty, the smaller cars were available sporting superbly appointed coachwork in open, closed and limousine guises. Typically closed cars offered foot-rails, smoker's companions, folding picnic tables, carpets and over-rugs. Cars with glass divisions routinely included speaking-tubes connecting passengers to driver, finely-upholstered folding occasional seats and/or oddments bins and cocktail cabinets. Luggage grids were available at the rear or on the roof, since most inter-axle space became passenger accommodation.

A Mark II version arrived in July, 1925, when the Standard wheelbase became 10'9", and in the following March the Short 18 reverted to the 10' wheelbase, when the 10'9" Standard version became the Long. A new monobloc engine with bores of 73mm and stroke of 114.29mm displaced 2872cc, and retained the vaned flywheel for cooling and gravity feed for fuel delivery. The Short used all semi-elliptic springs, while the Long used rear cantilevers, and both toured at 50mph.

William Morris (later Lord Nuffield) wrote in January, 1926 that "After having personally driven this car (*a Short 18*) over our test route, I can say that I know of few cars selling at £450 that compete with it for all round value. It struck me as being an excellent top gear performer – robust, substantial, and lively on acceleration".

Company publicist W.G. McMinnies ramped up the sales rhetoric with advertising copy like: "This Six is no respecter of gradients, for hidden in its shapely bonnet are half a hundred horses that wait your word to flatten out the steepest hill and send the milestones scuttling home". McMinnies was always noted for hyperbole.

Central chassis lubrication was fitted to the Short 18 from June, 1927 and was then extended to all models except the Twelve. For the 1928 season both wheelbase lengths were known as the 20hp.

The four-speed preselector gearbox available for an extra £35 from late 1928 was welcomed by drivers, even though that original 'self-change' transmission still required careful handling for sweet take-off and changes. Drive on the preselector 'box was taken up on the transmission bands, without a separate clutch, but it heralded the days of fully automatic gearchanging thanks to its employment of epicyclic gears. The comparative ease of operation was a showroom drawcard responsible for many sales in the late 1920s and early 1930s, when there was no competitor. The Special 20hp was optionally available with the Daimler-sourced fluid flywheel from late 1930 until late 1933, when supplies were denied to Armstrong Siddeley. Alvis introduced its all-synchromesh gearbox in 1932, but general use of such transmissions came 20-30 years later; the widespread availability of fully automatic gearboxes awaited the 1960s.

In November, 1928 an improved engine arrived – the monobloc six now sporting a cross-flow cylinder head – when it propelled the car to almost 70mph. The 18- and 20hp were compact and affordable six-cylinder touring cars, and sold strongly from the outset. Siddeley had correctly predicted that the post-war market for large and expensive cars would be short-lived, as the Thirty's sales quickly dwindled. Some 470 Eighteens sold in 1922, and 834 in 1923.

Owners' opinions quoted in company promotional literature included: "It may interest you to know that last week-end I climbed Honister Pass from the Buttermere side in the Short 18 saloon with five up. The pass is reputed to be 1-in-3 to 1-in-4 with about 12" of loose metal. It is marked at the bottom by the A.A. as being impracticable to motorists". The Editor of *The Motor* in England commissioned a special Short 20 fabric saloon from Hoyal Body Corporation, confirming his

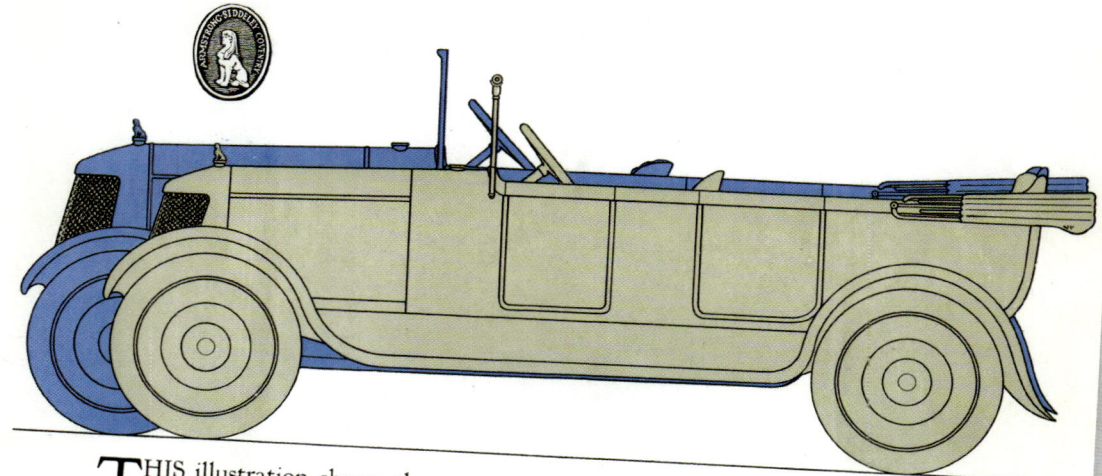

THIS illustration shows the comparative sizes of the 30 h.p. Armstrong Siddeley 6 Cylinder (in blue) and the new 18 h.p. Armstrong Siddeley 6 Cylinder (in grey).

endorsement of the cars which he had road tested.

Testament to the soundness of the 1921 design was the introduction of the New Twenty late in 1931, which in developing form sustained the upper end of the company's range until war's outbreak.

With an engine capacity increased to 3190cc, the New Twenty was fitted with a crankshaft vibration damper, coil ignition and belt-driven fan. Under-trays initially directed airflow around the motor and thermostatically-controlled radiator shutters were fitted, but although early examples eschewed bonnet louvres, they were installed after overheating was suffered with the new arrangement.

The principal departure from its predecessors was a completely new chassis. Its lowered frame provided a wheelbase of 10' 2½" in Short form, and 10' 11 ½" when in Long.form. All-round semi-elliptic springing, Luvax dampers and the option of steel discs or Magna wire wheels produced a revitalised specification.

Announcing the new model, *The Motor* of October 6, 1931 said: "This increase in engine size, together with a number of refinements in the combustion chambers and porting arrangements, has resulted

Below: Offside of the 18hp engine, showing the similarity of its design to the 30hp, with separate blocks and cylinder heads, external pushrod tubes, and gear-driven water pump and magneto.

Below right: Nearside of the 18hp engine, once again showing similar treatment of carburettor position, heated inlet manifold and the dynamo.

in a greatly increased power output at all rates of revolution speed, and in consequence the performance of the car on the road has been remarkably improved".

While the engine was fundamentally similar to its predecessor, the new chassis was reportedly lighter, producing an improved ratio of power to weight. Since the 1932 Rally Tourer weighed 33cwt (1676kg) and the 1934 Sports Saloon 1934 scaled 38cwt (1930kg) they were still not lightweights. But the Short Twenty was tested at 75mph, with 55mph available on third and 31mph on second – highly respectable speeds for a three-litre car in the early 1930s. The 0-50mph sprint took just 16.8 seconds, while fuel consumption typically bettered 20mpg. The heavier Long Twenty topped 70mph, and ran from 0-60mph in 29 seconds.

Subjected to regular updates, the New Twenty was in 1932 fitted with DWS permanent jacks and the Lucas Startix mechanism, while the updraught Claudel Hobson carburettor was changed to a downdraught variety, and with modified manifolding produced further improvements in power and sweet-running.

Also in 1932 the company entered three mildly modified New Twenty special-bodied two-seaters in the Alpine Trial, one driven by motoring journalist and racing driver S. C. H. 'Sammy' Davis. All cars used fan assemblies modified for better cooling, but these all failed and required repair. Neither this nor other faults occurring during the Trial denied each a Glacier Cup for penalty-free runs. The company acknowledged the value of such competition for product development, and considered entering a team of Siddeley Specials at LeMans, but was dissuaded from doing so by Sammy Davis.

The New Twenty continued to attract praise from motoring writers, *The Motor* on May 31, 1932 saying: "A few miles at the wheel convince one that here is a car of rare verve, capable of a high maximum speed, but most of all an excellent average over long distances...

"One is used to no-trouble cars in these days, but it is difficult to imagine any car which would give more pleasure for less effort than the new 20hp sports Armstrong Siddeley saloon".

The Editor of *The Motor*, who owned a special-bodied Twenty in 1928, bought a New Twenty and described it thus on December 10, 1933: "...I begin to praise this 20hp Armstrong Siddeley sports saloon, which is my modern magic carpet that takes me swiftly and silently to the coast and back in an easy daylight drive in mid-winter".

Coachwork offered on the New Twenty continued previous lines for the Long 20, but essayed some enterprising new directions on the shorter chassis. The Burlington-built sports sedan was a handsome four-light design with much-praised concealed luggage locker in its short tail, a style replicated in Australia by Creswell of Sydney. Many outside coachbuilders bodied short chassis cars, including Gill All-Weather Bodies Ltd, Charlesworth, Cunard Motor & Carriage Co (notable for their lavish 40/50hp Napiers), Palmers (Dover) Ltd,

Maltby, H J Mulliner, Salmons Tickford and James Young.

On the longer frame some more traditionally-inclined builders including Gurney Nutting, Hooper and Windovers produced exquisite carriages emphasising luxury over performance, while a superb St George's Sporting Saloon was created by Martin Walter – a four-light design on the longer frame. This handsome car pre-dated the long-running saloon built by Park Ward for the Derby Bentleys, and included many of its features including draught excluders, the shapely tail and the externally-mounted spare wheel with metal cover. Inside were vanity cabinets and smoker's companions, and a fitted hand-tool tray within a folding picnic table.

The New Twenty underwent major modification in June, 1936, evolving into the 20/25. The engine was enlarged to 3670cc with bores of 82.5mm, and carburation changed from Claudel Hobson to a side-draught SU. Power lifted to 85bhp at 3600rpm, allowing even the Long limousine to exceed 70mph and accelerate to 50mph in 20.2 seconds, despite its weight of 41cwt; a Short sports saloon was tested at 78.95mph and gave 66mph on third. Major revisions to the chassis produced reinforcing box-sections along its length, strengthened by three fabricated and three tubular cross-members.

From early 1937, the Newton-designed centrifugal clutch became standard, along with connection of engine and transmission styled as Balanced Drive, and Bendix duo-servo cable-operated brakes – changes applied first to the smaller-engined cars then ultimately across the model range. A sub-frame supported the engine, its apex beneath the radiator, its legs abreast of the bell housing. This sub-frame was rubber-insulated and the engine was rubber mounted, prompting *The Motor* to observe: "Good stability has been secured, so that the car rides steadily and feels safe, and the insulation afforded against road shocks is of a very high order".

From late 1938 the model name changed to the 25hp, and a fourth frame length was added, employing a wheelbase of 12 feet, onto which imperial limousines and specialist semi-commercial bodies like ambulances and large vans were built. Independent coachbuilders including Charlesworth, the Mayfair Carriage Co Ltd, H J Mulliner, Salmons and Windovers produced some handsomely proportioned bodies in the elegant flowing mode of the late 1930s, which were a fitting end to the long production life beginning as Armstrong Siddeley's second product in 1921.

Left: 18hp chassis, displaying its torque tube drive, gearbox mounted at its front end, and the diagonally-braced rear axle. As for the 30hp, the running boards were affixed to the chassis side-members, thereby assisting their rigidity.

ARMSTRONG SIDDELEY

FINEST VALUE IN FINE CARS

Olympia: Stand 178

¶ During the show a complete display of all types will be on view at 10 Old Bond St., W.1

The Equipment includes everything desirable in a high-class motor carriage

ARMSTRONG SIDDELEY MOTORS LIMITED, COVENTRY,
(Allied with Sir W. G. Armstrong Whitworth & Co., Ltd.),
London: 10 Old Bond St., W.1.   Manchester: 35 King St. West
Agents in all principal centres.   Service Depots at Coventry,
London, Manchester, Newcastle, Leeds, Bristol and Glasgow

1924 PRICES.

		£
FOUR Cylinder 14 h.p.	Chassis fully equipped	260
	2 Seater with Dickey	360
	Standard Open Touring Car	360
	do do (with special equipment)	385
	Saloon	480
	Saloon Landaulette	505
SIX Cylinder 18 h.p.	Chassis, fully equipped	480
	5 Seater Open Touring Car, completely equipped (including rear screen, luggage grid, etc.)	670
	Saloon	765
	Landaulette	820
	Enclosed Limousine or Landaulette	860
SIX Cylinder 30 h.p.	Chassis, fully equipped	700
	5 Seater Open Touring Car, completely equipped (including rear screen, luggage grid, etc.)	950
	Landaulette or Limousine	1125
	Enclosed Landaulette or Limousine	1250

¶ Front Wheel Brakes can be supplied to 30 h.p. models at an extra cost of £35.

YOU . CANNOT . BUY . A . BETTER . CAR

Open tourer by Burlington, first series.

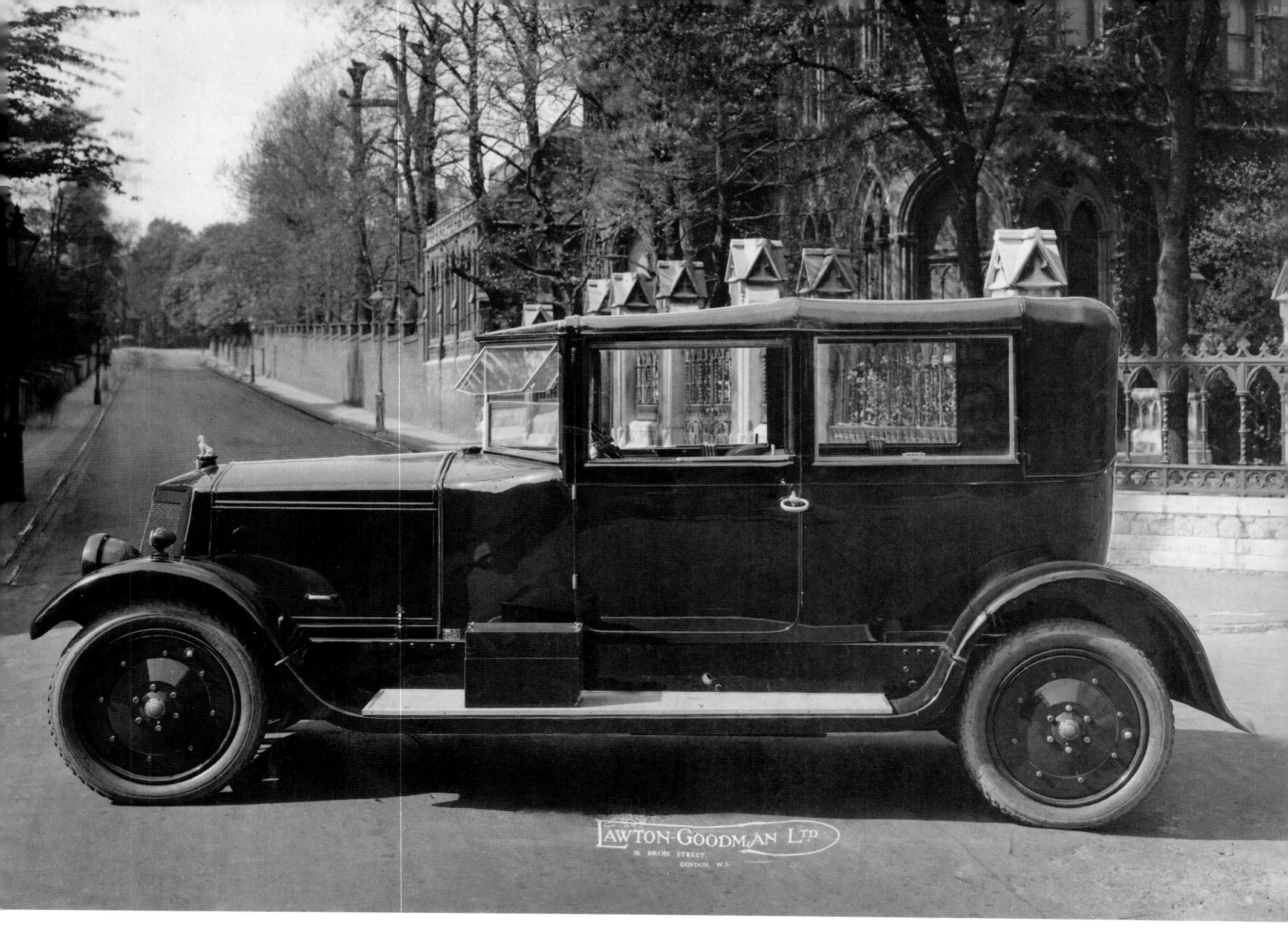

Handsome vee-screen two door saloon bodied by Lawton Goodman, London.

Mann Egerton built this enclosed landaulette on the 18hp chassis in 1924.

Harrods Private Car Hire Service

This 18 h.p. Armstrong-Siddeley Saloon-Landaulet exclusively at your Service for £60 a month.

Though of smaller power this Car yields nothing in finish and equipment to the higher-powered Cars shown on the preceding pages.

The body is finished in Harrods own carriage works and provides ample accommodation for five passengers.

The Car is electrically lighted, velvet-smooth in running, and in every respect of superlative quality and appearance.

The exceptional wheel-lock makes this model specially suitable for use in traffic.

On a yearly contract reckoning on a mileage not exceeding 9000 miles the charge for this Car inclusive of Harrods full Service is £60 a month.

HARRODS LTD   6   *LONDON SW 1*

30

A Harrods private car service garage in Draycott Avenue Chelsea SW.

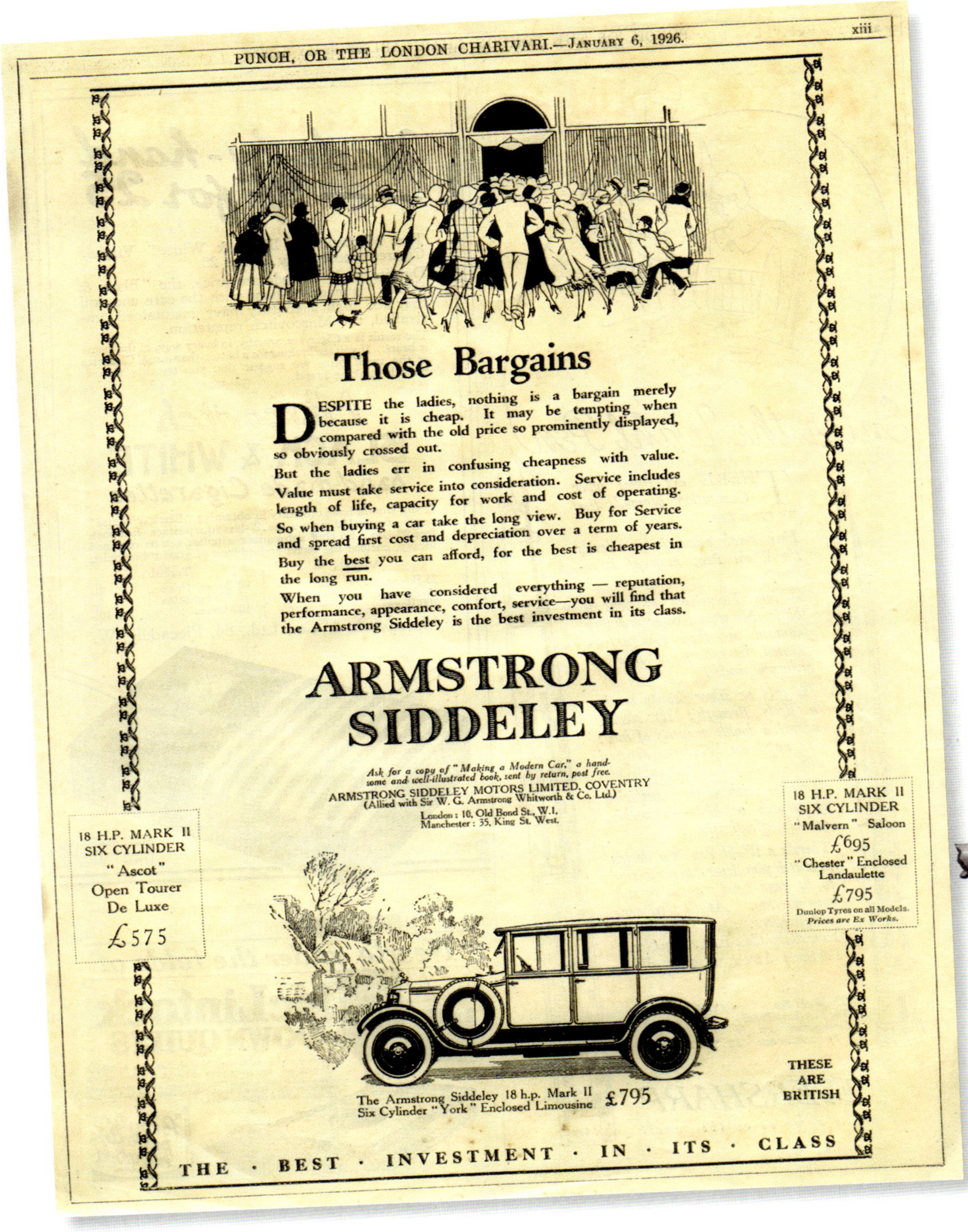

PUNCH, OR THE LONDON CHARIVARI.—January 6, 1926. xiii

Those Bargains

DESPITE the ladies, nothing is a bargain merely because it is cheap. It may be tempting when compared with the old price so prominently displayed, so obviously crossed out.

But the ladies err in confusing cheapness with value. Value must take service into consideration. Service includes length of life, capacity for work and cost of operating. So when buying a car take the long view. Buy for Service and spread first cost and depreciation over a term of years. Buy the best you can afford, for the best is cheapest in the long run.

When you have considered everything — reputation, performance, appearance, comfort, service—you will find that the Armstrong Siddeley is the best investment in its class.

ARMSTRONG SIDDELEY

Ask for a copy of "Making a Modern Car," a handsome and well-illustrated book, sent by return, post free.

ARMSTRONG SIDDELEY MOTORS LIMITED, COVENTRY
(Allied with Sir W. G. Armstrong Whitworth & Co. Ltd.)

London: 10, Old Bond St., W.1.
Manchester: 35, King St. West.

18 H.P. MARK II
SIX CYLINDER
"Ascot"
Open Tourer
De Luxe
£575

18 H.P. MARK II
SIX CYLINDER
"Malvern" Saloon
£695
"Chester" Enclosed
Landaulette
£795
Dunlop Tyres on all Models.
Prices are Ex Works.

The Armstrong Siddeley 18 h.p. Mark II Six Cylinder "York" Enclosed Limousine £795

THESE ARE BRITISH

THE · BEST · INVESTMENT · IN · ITS · CLASS

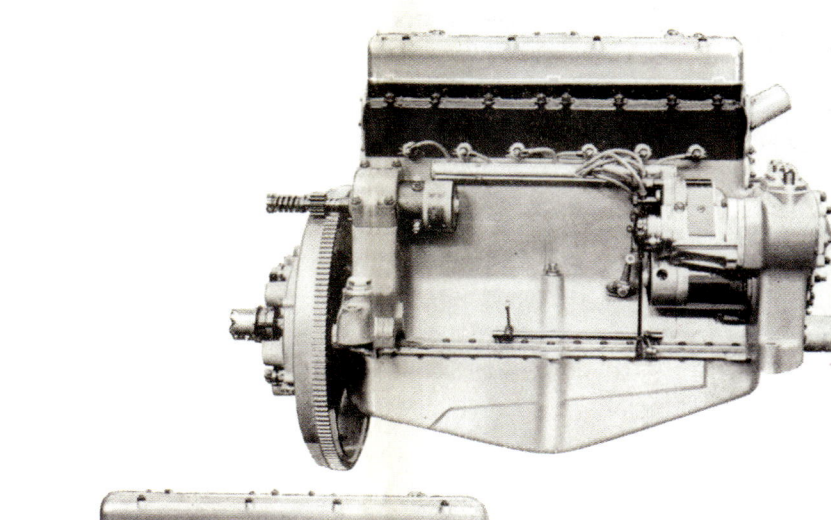

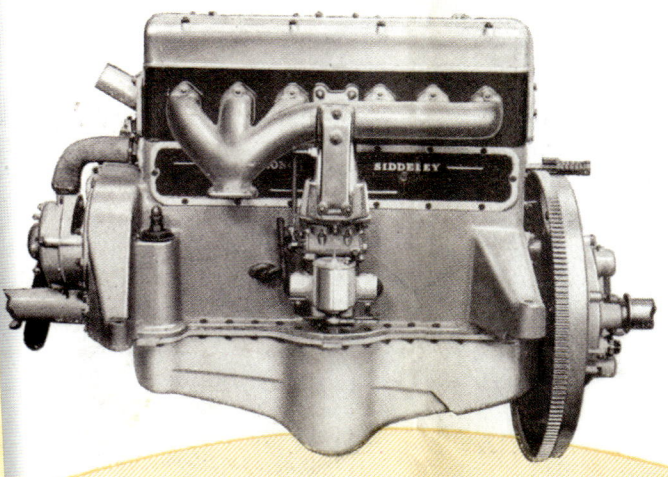

Above (upper): Offside view of the much cleaner architecture of the Mark II 18hp motor, noting that it is now of monobloc construction.
Above (lower): Nearside view, showing retention of the updraught Claudel Hobson carburettor and flywheel fan.

Burlington built a wide range of bodies on the 18hp, even though some of them were produced in only handfuls. Here is the Maidstone saloon-landaulette on the Long Mark II chassis.

Above: The Burlington-built Arundel
2-3 seater on the Short chassis.

Right: The Taunton open tourer.

Above: The stately Stirling Saloon.

Left: The Braemar Special Tourer – note the rear screen, and the front-opening front doors – unusual in the late 1920s, even though common in the 1930s.

Above: The lightweight Cranwell Fabric Saloon on the Short chassis.

Right: Burlington's Eaton Special Saloon. The 'Special' features were lavish interior fittings.

Above: The Carlisle Three-Quarter Landaulette – quite late for open-sided chauffeur-driven motor cars.

Left: The Conway Saloon Landaulette on the Long chassis.

Above: From 1928 the 18/20hp was available with the four-speed preselective Wilson gearbox at extra cost. This clever promotional item from that year purports to instruct drivers in the principles of the new system.

Right: The smart Harlech dickey-seat coupé on the Short frame.

Long 18hp and period caravan, outside the Martin Walter coachbuilding works in Folkestone, 1922.

Above: Mark II open tourer, bodied by Burlington, 1927.

Left: Charming period photograph of a Burlington-bodied late 18hp saloon.

Armstrong Siddeley Touring Fabric Saloon

With Triplex glass throughout.

14 h.p. FOUR CYLINDERS - £385
15 h.p. SIX CYLINDERS - - £415
20 h.p. SIX CYLINDERS - £495

Self-changing Silent Four Speed Gear £35 extra.
(20 h.p. only).

Above: The 20hp fabric Touring Saloon was the successor to the close-coupled 'Sociable' body style applied to the 30hp. It was available on the 14hp, 15hp and 20hp chassis.

Opposite page: 20hp saloon bodied by Ruskin of Melbourne, Australia. The style shows the strong American influence on Australian coachbuilding of the time. Many companies built clones of American bodies on American chassis, and simply applied them to British and European makes.

THE EDITORIAL TWENTY

"Since last March quarter day the editorial Armstrong Siddeley Twenty has done 14,000 miles. The top speed seems to be about 75 m.p.h. and its nicest cruising speed between 60 and 65 m.p.h. At that it just sits on the road and purrs and is a great deal more comfortable than any Pullman car. It can always do 40 and on anything like open roads it does 50 miles in the hour easily.

Its extraordinary performance on corners and in traffic is largely due to the Wilson gear box with the pre-selector gear. I have driven this gear box for three years and have deliberately used it brutally. And in something over 35,000 miles not a thing has gone wrong."

C. G. GREY, *Editor of "The Aeroplane."*

ARMSTRONG SIDDELEY

Write for Catalogue "L. 432"

Armstrong Siddeley Motors Limited, Coventry.   10, Old Bond Street, London, W.1.   35, King Street West, Manchester

BP432G

THE TWENTY H.P. SPORTS SALOON

ALSO FITTED TO THE NEW 17 H.P. CHASSIS.

THIS MODEL REPRESENTS THE MOST DISTINCTIVE AND MODERN BODY OF ITS CLASS. WHILST IT POSSESSES SPORTING LINES, IT HAS RETAINED THAT ESSENTIAL DIGNITY WHICH DIFFERENTIATES ARMSTRONG SIDDELEY CARS FROM THE USUAL TYPE OF SPORTS CAR. THE INTERNAL FURNISHING OF PERFECT HARMONY AND TASTE, GIVES THE UTMOST COMFORT WITH PLENTY OF LEG AND HEAD ROOM. THE LUGGAGE ACCOMMODATION IS AMPLE FOR ALL REASONABLE REQUIREMENTS. COLOURS ARE :—BLUE, GREY, GREEN, CREAM AND BLACK. LEATHER TO MATCH.

17 H.P. £495 £585 20 H.P.

10

The New 20hp Sports Saloon broke new ground for Armstrong Siddeley and the Burlington coachbuilder, offering a modern new appearance, comfortable between-axle seating and concealed rear luggage compartment.

THE TWENTY H.P. CHASSIS

THE CLEAN, IMPRESSIVE DESIGN OF THE TWENTY HORSE-POWER CHASSIS, ITS DEEP FRAME OF BOX SECTION — PERFECTLY BRACED TO WITHSTAND ALL STRESSES — THE PROVED SELF-CHANGE GEAR; THE HIGHLY EFFICIENT ENGINE — GIVING MAXIMUM POWER — FREE FROM ALL UNNECESSARY COMPLICATIONS AND WITH EVERY PART READILY ACCESS-IBLE, PROCLAIMS ITSELF TO BE OF THAT UNCOMMON QUALITY WHICH DISTINGUISHES THE HANDWORK OF SIDDELEY AERO-ENGINEERS. IT PROVIDES A STANDARD OF PERFORMANCE-FOR-POWER OF UNEQUALLED MERIT, WHICH IS MAINTAINED FOR LONG PERIODS.

8

Although the coachbuilder of this very specially equipped Sports Saloon is not confirmed, the front-opening front doors suggest Burlington. The roof-mounted searchlamp, polished wheel discs and tubular bumpers are stylish additions to the usual 1933 specification.

THE TWENTY LIMOUSINE

TO PROVIDE FOR THE ELABORATE COACHWORK OF A LIMOUSINE OR LANDAULETTE WITH FULLY ENCLOSED DRIVE, A LONGER CHASSIS IS PROVIDED. THE DRIVING COMPARTMENT IS FURNISHED WITH GREAT COMFORT AND THE OCCASIONAL EXTRA SEATS ARE DESIGNED TO GIVE REAL EASE. SPECIAL ATTENTION HAS BEEN GIVEN TO THE FINISH AND APPOINTMENTS. AN ATMOSPHERE OF LUXURY AND ELEGANCE HAS BEEN CREATED — CORRECT IN EVERY DETAIL AND, IN FASHION, ADAPTED TO THE MOST FORMAL OCCASIONS. COLOURS TO CHOICE.

£745

9

Delivery day for Sydney doctor, C Eden-George, of his 1934 20hp with Burlington Sports Saloon coachwork. The Lucas P80 headlamps, stainless bumpers and chrome-plated wheels were all special features of this handsome car.

Above: This open two-seater roadster body was available on both the Long 15 and the Short 20 chassis.

Opposite page: Burlington saloon body on the late New 20 Long chassis.

Right: 20hp Sports Saloon illustrated by the factory with emphasis on the marque's attachment to successful aircraft, for which they built engines or complete aeroplanes.

Below: The Armstrong Siddeley stand at the 1932 Olympia Motor Show, with New 20 chassis and (at left) Sports Saloon featured.

Opposite page: Most handsome close-coupled coachbuilt New 20 competing in a hill-climb event, 1932.

Brochure illustration of the Burlington Rally Tourer body, available on both the Long 15 and the Short 20 chassis.

The handsome Atalanta body style was introduced on the 17hp in late 1936, and in expanded form was applied to the larger cars. This 1938 example was offered for £625.

The 25hp Coach Saloon was a more formal design that sold for £575.

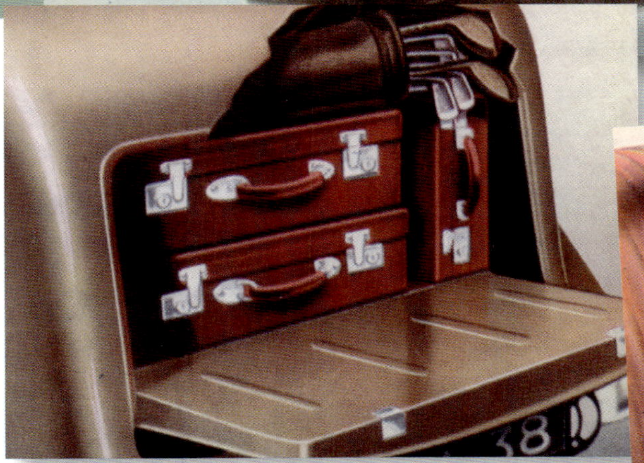

The 25hp Touring Saloon was notable for its extended luggage compartment, proudly described as being able to accommodate two sets of golf clubs. It sold for £575.

The 25hp was available on the longest wheelbase
with sumptuous limousine or landaulette coachwork,
as shown in this brochure image.

Period image of the C Allen & Son service depot, Whitelands Road, Bristol, in around 1935.
The breakdown vehicle appears to be a late Mark II 20hp Armstrong Siddeley, with crane attachment.

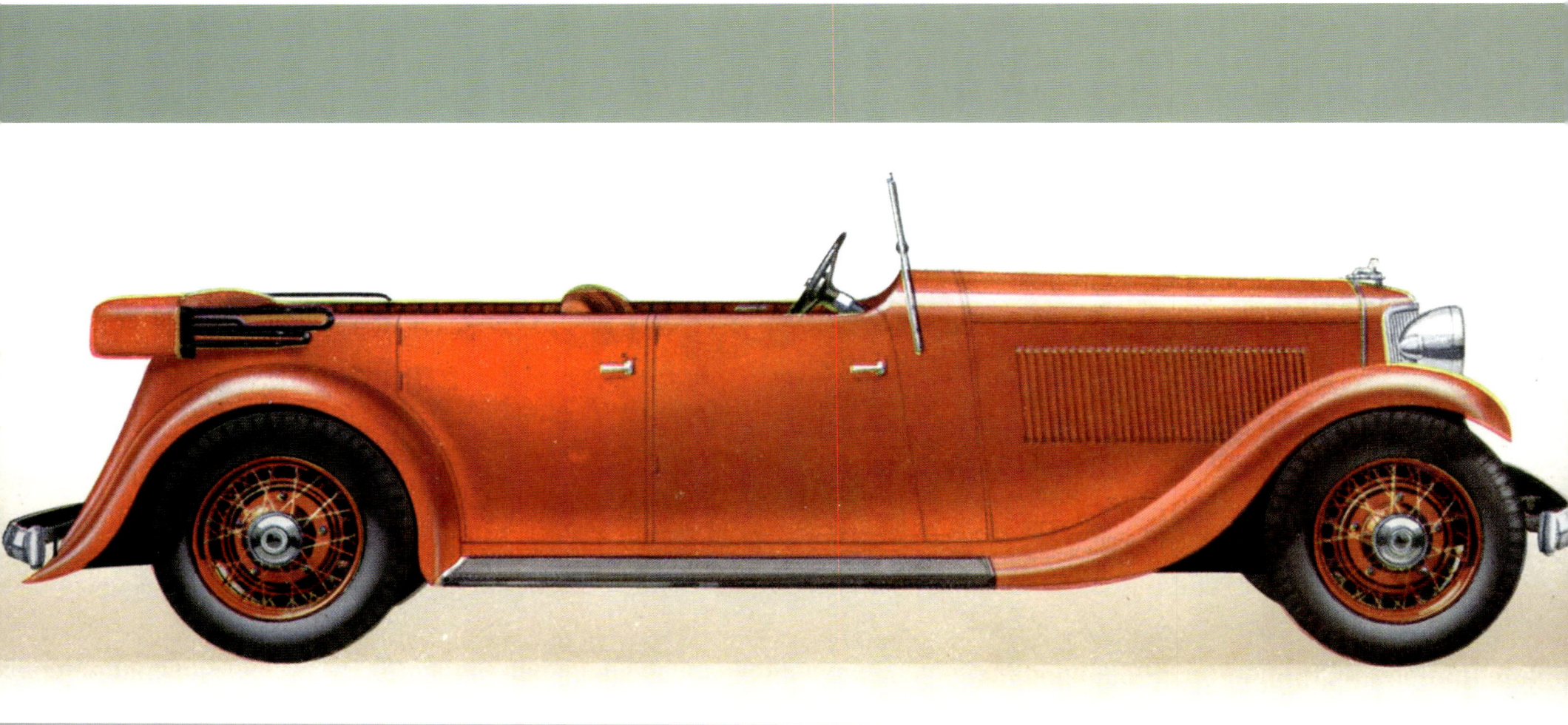

This striking open four-seat tourer was made available by Burlington
on both the Long 17 and the 20/25hp chassis.

Late 20/25 or 25hp bodied as a shooting brake, but coachbuilder unknown.

Above: The 25hp Town & Country
Saloon was an attempt to provide one
car that could fulfil formal and informal
roles, its glass division capable of being
wound down when driven by other
than a chauffeur.

Insets: Interior detail of the 25hp Town
& Country Saloon.

Left: Very late 25hp ambulance built on the longest of the three chassis lengths available for that model. The coachbuilder is unknown.

Factory designation	18hp	18hp Mark II/20hp	New 20hp
Date introduced	November 1921	March 1925	August 1931
Motor type	6 cyl 4-stroke in-line water-cooled bi-bloc ohv	monobloc ohv	same
Dimensions	69.5 X 104.8mm = 2380cc	73 X 114.29mm = 2872cc	73 X 127mm = 3190cc
Power/rpm	17.9hp RAC rating	20hp RAC rating	
Fuel feed	gravity to dual-choke updraught Claudel Hobson carb	same	Mech pump & downdraught Claudel Hobson carb
Ignition	BTH magneto	same	battery & coil, Lucas Startix
Transmission type	3-speeds & rev crash gearbox	4-spd & rev Wilson 'box option on 20hp mid 1928	4-spd & rev preselector 'box standardised
Ratios	16.65 7.82 4.7:1 Rev 23.8:1	same	(Short)18.45 10.37 6.19 4.1:1 Rev (Long) 19.8 11.13 6.63.4.4:1
Final drive ratio	4.7:1 spiral bevel rear axle	same	(Short) 4.1:1 (Long) 4.4:1 spiral bevel drive axle
Clutch	single dry plate	same	none, but Daimler Fluid Flywheel optional
Steering	worm & wheel, adjustable for rake	same	worm & nut
Suspension			
Front	gaitered semi-elliptic springs	same	same with Luvax dampers
Rear	gaitered cantilevers adjustable for height	same	underslung semi-elliptics, Luvax dampers
Brakes	2-whl brakes (rear) 17½" drums operated by rods	4-whl 17½" drums operated by rods	Bendix semi-servo operated by cables
Wheels	steel disc wheels	same	same, bolt-on wires optional
Tyres	815X105mm	820X120 or 5.25X31"	(Short) 5.50 X 19" (Long) 6.00 X 18"
Dimensions			
Wheelbase	10'	(Short) 10', (Standard) 10'9"	(Short) 10'2½" (Long) 10'11½"
Track front	4'3"	(Short) 4'8", (Standard) 4'6"	(Short & Long) 4'8"
Track rear	same as front	same as front	same as front
Overall length	dependent on body-style & coachbuilder	(Short) 13'2", (Standard) 13'9"	(Short) 14'6" (Long) 15'2" (+12" for opt bumpers)
Overall width	5'4"	(Short) 5'6", (Standard) 5'4"	(Short & Long) 5'9"
Height	dependent on body-style & coachbuilder	same	Rally tourer 5'9½"
Unladen weight			33cwt (Rally tourer) 38cwt (Sports saloon)
Factory coachwork	open tourer, saloon, landaulette	tourer, slaoon, ¾ & enclosed landaulette/limousine	coachbuilt & sports saloons, Rally tourer, limo
Variants	per outside coachbuilders	same	same
Performance			
Max speed (mph)	55-60	60	73
Fuel consumption (mpg)	21-24	(Short) 22-24; (Standard) 21	17-20
Number produced	2126	(Short) 5067, (Standard) 1574	(Short) 1951 (Long) 698
Prices	chassis £575, tourer £795, saloon £895, landaulette £975	(1925) chassis Short £350; Standard £450 (1927) tourer £435, saloon £525, 2/3 seater £450, landaulette & coupé £550, Std saloon £695 Std encl landaulette £795, fabric saloon 20hp £495	Rally tourer £535, sports saloon £565, saloon £575, Long limousine or landaulette £745,
Date last produced	1925	(Short) July 1931 (Standard) October 1931	(Short) December 1935 (Long) March 1936

Factory designation	20/25	25hp
Date introduced	(short) June 1936 (long) May 1936	June 1937
Motor type	6 cyl 4-stroke in line water-cooled ohv	same
Dimensions	82.5 X 114mm = 3670cc	same
Power/rpm	85bhp @ 3600rpm	same
Fuel feed	mechanical pump from rear tank to SU side-draught carb	same
Ignition	battery & coil with automatic control	same
Transmission type	Wilson 4-spd & Rev preselective	same, but in unit with engine
Ratios	(short) 14.54 8.46 5.57 4.09:1 (long) 16.7 9.7 6.4 4.7:1	(Short) 15.51 9.02 5.94 4.36:1
		(long) 16.7 9.7 6.4 4.7:1
Final drive ratio	(short) 4.09:1 (long) 4.7:1) spiral bevel axle	(short) 4.36:1 (Long) 4.7:1
Clutch	single dry plate connected to gearbox	automatic centrifugal dry plate (from June 1936)
Steering	worm & nut	same
Suspension		
Front	gaitered semi-elliptic springs, Luvax dampers	same
Rear	underslung semi-elliptic springs, Luvax dampers	same
Brakes	4-wheel semi-servo	same
Wheels	(short) 17" steel disc (long) 18" steel disc, bolt on wires optional	same
Tyres	(short) 6.00 X 17" (long) 6.50 X 18"	same
Dimensions		
Wheelbase	(short) 10'3" (long) 10'11"	same
Track front	(short & long) 4'8"	same but (long) 4'9"
Track rear	(short) 4'9" (long) 4'10"	same but (long) 5'0"
Overall length (incl bumpers)	(short) 15'10" (long) 16'7"	(short) 15'6" (long) 15'9"
Overall width	(short) 5'9" (long) 5'10"	same
Height	(short) 5'9", otherwise dependent on body style and coachbuilder	same
Unladen weight	(short) 35cwt (long) 41cwt, otherwise dependent on body style and coachbuilder	same
Factory coachwork	6-lt touring saloon, 4-lt Atalanta saloon, 7-seat limousine or landaulette	touring saloon, coachbuilt saloon, town & country
		saloon, Atalanta saloon, limousine/landaulette
Variants	per outside coachbuilders	same
Performance		
Max speed (mph)	(short) 81 (long) 72 (note shorter final drive gearing)	same
Fuel consumption (mpg)	(short) 16-18	same
Number produced (total)	(short) 447 (long) 445	
Prices	6-lt touring saloon £575, 4-lt Atalanta saloon £625,	same plus coachbuilt saloon £575,
	limousine or landaulette £745	town & country saloon £595
Date last produced		(short) December 1939 (long) January 1940

THE STONELEIGH EXPERIMENT
1921-1924

The Armstrong Siddeley-built Stoneleigh was a classic case of the wrong car at the wrong time. Before the first war the Deasy Motor Car Manufacturing Company, with Siddeley as Managing Director and General Manager, opted to produce a basic motor car priced within reach of those who may have otherwise been restricted to a motorcycle and sidecar for family transport. Wisely the Directors wished to separate this type of vehicle from their established image as producers of quality motor carriages, and incorporated Stoneleigh Motors Limited in June, 1912, specifically to build light cars and commercial vehicles.

The original Stoneleigh light car was a cloned BSA 13.9hp chassis, separated from its progenitor only by its coachwork and badging. Its two-litre Knight sleeve valve engine was identical and its two-year guarantee was honoured by BSA, not Deasy. The little car was a full four-seater with four doors, and was driven via a rear-mounted transaxle. Contemporary reports placed its maximum speed at 35mph, although 25mph was deemed more comfortable.

In the two years before the onset of war, the company also built two light trucks before encouraging its workforce to enlist and closing its

doors. However an unexpected order from the Russian Government for 100 light trucks forced a rapid re-think. Production was resumed of trucks and field kitchens for the Russian front, and later included for other theatres aero engines and complete aircraft. But that's another story. Although the BSA continued in production through 1914, the original Stoneleigh light car was built for barely 12 months; none is known to survive.

Upon the advent of Armstrong Siddeley Motors Limited in 1919, Siddeley first built his large and imperious 30hp, then quickly turned his attention to additional market segments as ultimately filled by the 18hp, 14hp and a reinvigorated Stoneleigh. The new version bore scant resemblance to its predecessor, being conceived as a 3-seater powered by an air-cooled vee-twin engine. Marketed first as a Utility (without the modern light commercial connotations), the little car's overhead valve motor had bores of 85mm with stroke of 88mm, displacing 998cc, with coil ignition. Its conventional gearbox had three speeds and, like the larger Parkside cars, was attached to the front end of the torque tube. However presumably for cost reasons a differential was not used. There were removable disc wheels, but brakes on the rear only.

Despite a wheelbase of 8' and an overall length of 10'9", Siddeley's approval of a central driving position in the front, with a single bench behind, simply beggars belief. Spin of the day declared that "...the driver's attention will not be distracted by nervous or talkative passengers", although quite why they should be mute when travelling on the rear seat is not revealed. The rear bench was easily removed to carry goods during the week or replaced for passengers at the weekend.

It was suspended on quarter elliptic springs which, without the assistance of shock absorbers, produced handling much like the later Alvis front-wheel drive car – similarly suspended – which according to one observer "went around corners in a series of wobbles".

While intended as 'no frills' basic family transport, the Stoneleigh was widely derided by factory workers as 'the washtub', the 'sack of potatoes car', and Siddeley as "the man who made walking a pleasure".

The car was competitively priced at £185 fully equipped with hood, spare wheel, bulb horn and lighting set, when the air-cooled Rover 8 cost £195. But Herbert Austin trumped the Stoneleigh at the 1922 Olympia Motor Show with his new Seven, a four-seater powered by a famously lively water-cooled four-cylinder engine, three-speed gearbox and differential, and four wheel brakes. Proving that cheap need not mean nasty, it was the sensation of the Show, and immediately made offerings like the Stoneleigh appear ungainly and, at £30 more,

relatively expensive. At the same Show closed versions were exhibited but were not continued into production. Varying the fare a light delivery van body was offered on the Utility chassis, and could carry 4cwt, slowly.

For 1923 the curiously conceived Utility was joined by a more conventional four-seater right-hand drive Chummy at that year's Olympia Motor Show; the two cars were priced at £155 and £165 respectively, the Stoneleigh Chummy equalling the price of Austin's Seven. The Chummy's two rear seats could be folded up to allow the carriage of luggage or goods as required.

Stoneleighs participated in some highly-publicised trials, most notably the Royal Scottish Automobile Club's 1000-mile Light Car Trial in June, 1922, when one of the two cars entered won a Gold Medal. In December, 1922, two Stoneleighs competed in the London-Exeter Trial, both winning Gold Medals. A silver medal was awarded to factory employee Douglas Yeats-Smith in the Colmore Cup Trial for light cars to 1100cc, and in October, 1923 the same driver drove a Chummy up the Snowdon Mountain railway; exactly why is not recorded, but the achievement was greeted with communal yawns from the motoring press.

Production continued into 1924, but it is hard to imagine that this ponderous car could compete with the likes of the Austin, despite its marginal superiority to the crop of cycle-cars which sold for not very much less. Probably fewer than 400 were produced between 1921 and 1924.

Right: Brochure image of the Stoneleigh Utility, with centre steering and single front seat. The rear bench could be folded or removed to allow load carrying.

Top right: Plan of the Utility, explaining why in the Armstrong Siddeley works it was known as the 'washtub'.

The Stoneleigh Three-Seater . . . . £155.

The Stoneleigh " Chummy " Model . . . . £165.

Above: The Chummy model, with conventional steering and four seats.

Far right: Plan view of the Chummy, showing its two front seats and occasional rears.

Right: The sparse facia of both Stoneleigh models provided little information for the driver.

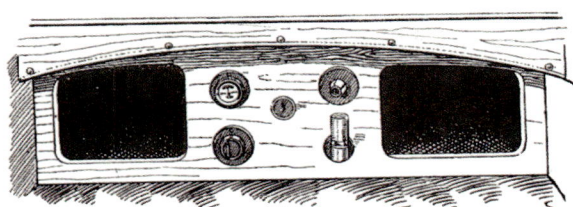

The Stoneleigh Instrument Board.

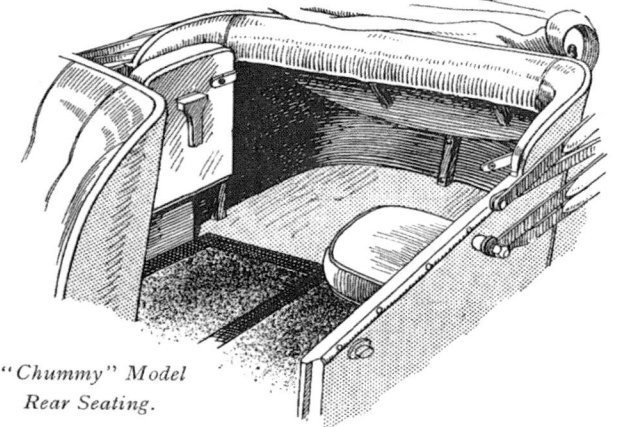

"Chummy" Model Rear Seating.

Above: The rear seats on the Chummy folded up to allow the carriage of loads when not required for (small) passengers.

Right: The Stoneleigh Chummy preserved by the Rolls-Royce Heritage Trust.

PW 1818

Factory designation	Stoneleigh Utility	Stoneleigh Chummy
Date introduced	April 1922	1923
Motor type	2 cyl 90° horizontally opposed ohv air-cooled	
Dimensions	85 X 88mm=998cc	
Power/rpm	8.9hp RAC rating, £9 tax	
Fuel feed	gravity feed to Claudel Hobson downdraught carburettor	
Ignition	dynamo & battery, Remy distributor	
Transmission type	3-speeds & reverse, crash	
Ratios	22 9.1 5:1 Rev 25.4:1	
Final drive ratio	5:1, no differential, spiral bevel drive	
Clutch	fabric single plate, fitted with clutch stop	
Steering	worm & segment	
Suspension	quarter-elliptic springs all round, no dampers	
Brakes	drums on rear wheels only	
Wheels	steel detachable discs	
Tyres	28 X 3" beaded edge	
Dimensions		
Wheelbase	8'0"	
Track front	4'0"	
Track rear	4'0"	
Overall length	10'9"	
Overall width	4'9"	
Height		
Unladen weight	10 cwt complete	
Factory coachwork	3-seater (front centre) 2-door open tourer	4-seater 2-door open tourer
Variants	saloon, coupé, van	
Performance		
Max speed (mph)	35	
Fuel consumption	not quoted, but factory literature boasted running costs of "less than three half-pence per mile"	
Number produced	364 total	
Price	1922: Utility £185 1923: Utility £155, Chummy £165	
Date last produced	October 1924	

JOHN DAVENPORT SIDDELEY A CAREER OVERVIEW

The working life of John Davenport Siddeley (JDS) was convoluted and wide-ranging. He began work in his family's hosiery business, then trained in engineering at Manchester Technical College. Beginning as a draughtsman with the Humber Cycle Company, his manufacturing work progressed to tyres, motor cars, aero engines, military hardware, cinematic projection equipment, railcars and complete aircraft.

The following timeline attempts to unravel the skeins of Siddeley's remarkable career:

1866 (Aug)	Born at Longsight, Manchester
1892	Joined Humber Cycle Co as designer-draughtsman
1893	Joined Pneumatic Tyre Co, Belfast
1898	Established Clipper Tyre Co, Coventry
1901	Became British importer of Peugeot cars
1902	Formed Siddeley Autocar Co, Coventry
1903	Through Vickers Sons & Maxim, owners of the Wolseley Sheep-Shearing Machine Co, built his first car
1905-6	Appointed Sales Manager, then General Manager, of the Wolseley Company – cars designed by him were named Wolseley-Siddeleys
1909	Appointed General Manager, then Managing Director, Deasy Motor Car Mfg Co, London, producing some Deasy and 'JDS Type Deasy' cars
1912	Formed Stoneleigh Motors Ltd for the purpose of dealing with the new light car and eventually with commercial vehicle business
1913	Acquired Burlington Carriage Company for in-house coachbuilding
1914	Built light trucks and ambulances for the Russian Front
1916	Commenced building aircraft engines and complete aircraft
1919	Under his direction, the Siddeley Deasy Motor Car Co was merged with the Sir W G Armstrong Whitworth Company, and in May the Sir W G Armstrong Whitworth Development Company was registered
1919 (Oct)	From that Company evolved Armstrong Siddeley Motors Ltd
1920	At his suggestion, a further subsidiary – Sir W G Armstrong Whitworth Aircraft Company – was formed specifically to build aircraft
1921	Registered Searchlight Projectors Ltd to manufacture mechanised film projection equipment
1921	Supervised construction of pilotless aircraft
1922	Supervised refinement, design and construction of specialist military prototypes, including a tracked personnel carrier
1923	Supplied engines for various Vickers Medium tanks, including those powered by Armstrong Siddeley-built 90bhp air-cooled V8 engines
1926	Elected to the Board of Armstrong Whitworth Development Company. Purchased that company in november, changing its name to Armstrong Siddeley Development Company
1927 (Feb)	Elected Chairman of that company
1928	With W G Wilson formed Improved Gears Ltd to manage manufacturing licences for the Wilson epicyclic gearbox
1928 (May)	Armstrong Siddeley Development Company acquired aircraft maker A V Roe and Company, and established High Duty Alloys after acquiring Peter Hooker Ltd
1932	Knighthood (C.B.E.) conferred for services to the mechanical development of the armed forces
1934	Established the Coventry Pneumatic Railcar Company to build pneumatic-tyred railcars, the first of which was completed in 1936*
1935	Sold his interests to Hawker Aircraft Company, which had also acquired the Gloster Company and Bristol Aeroplane Company. The new company became the Hawker Siddeley Aircraft Company Ltd
1936	Resigned as Chairman of Armstrong Siddeley Development Company
1937	Appointed Baron Kenilworth
1953	Died and buried in Jersey

* Two such railcars were built, powered by Armstrong Siddeley-designed and built 275bhp V12 petrol engines. Railway workers, noting their silence using rubber-shod wheels on metal tracks, named them *The Silent Death.*

For glimpses of JDS the man, I am heavily reliant on views and statements by former staffers of his various companies, contained in *The Evening and the Morning,* compiled in 1956 to record fifty years of manufacturing activity since the establishment of the Deasy Motor Car Co.

Siddeley is therein described as a 'holy terror' and 'a bit of a slave driver'. He was headstrong and determined to get his way, and knew what he wanted. He was noted from his earliest days as an outstanding organiser, with a clear view of the outcomes he required, and equally clear ideas on how to achieve them.

Armstrong Siddeley car development was constrained by his long-standing doggedness about such anachronisms as flywheel fans, and separately-mounted transmissions, which quickly disappeared upon his departure.

He was a ruthless autocrat and a gifted entrepreneur. He had the ability to think outside the square, and to accurately predict market trends. His flair led him to pursue the most marginal opportunities in hope of steering his companies in new and profitable directions, although ventures including the flickerless cinematic projector and the pneumatic-tyred railcar never achieved commercial success.

His common touch with his employees led him to establish staff cottages rented at less than market rates, convert an institute building into a Social Club and later a Church, establish a non-contributory staff benevolent fund, allow visits to nearby cities for movies and concerts, and foster the development of a male voice choir. While staff respected and perhaps feared him, he inspired long-term loyalty, and the three technicians he brought to The Deasy from Wolseley in 1909 stayed for the rest of their working lives.

By 1935 JDS was almost 70 years old, and despite early pride in knowing all his employees by name, this was now impossible as his workforce was approaching 2500. Toward the end of his incumbency he clashed repeatedly with engineers with new ideas, working within a whole new commercial landscape largely shaped by one world war and the threat of another.

Since he was widely regarded as 'a perfect gentleman' it is unfortunate that he appears to have outstayed his welcome at The Siddeley, and his departure to his beloved garden appears to have been greeted with relief. He purchased Kenilworth Castle as his residence, and immediately gifted it to the State.

There is no doubt that the conglomerate which proved so vital to England's defence in World War 2 was very largely the work of one man, whose uncompromising approach to anything he made meant that the lowliest or the most adventurous manufactured items were all built to the same high standards.

Armstrong Siddeley motor-cars remained true to his design philosophy to their very last model, the Star Sapphire, which many regard as the finest to carry the sphinx mascot.

John Davenport Siddeley reacquaints himself with a 1904 Siddeley Autocar in 1950.

CHAPTER iv

THE FOUR-FOURTEEN MARK I AND MARK II
1923-1929
AND THE FIFTEEN HP CARS
1927-1934

Introduced in May, 1923, the Fourteen was the company's first venture into a four-cylinder car, yet followed closely the pattern established by its larger six-cylinder brethren. This was Siddeley's means of extending the market appeal of his cars into the family sector, but in all respects the smaller car maintained the high manufacturing standards of the other models, and bore proudly the Armstrong Siddeley name and sphinx mascot. In the works the evolving new model was known as the "Stoneleigh Two", its radiator was flat rather than vee-shaped, angled rearwards at the top like that of the Armstrong Siddeley-built Stoneleigh, but there the similarity ended.

In common with the Thirty and Eighteen was its overhead valve motor, three speed crash gearbox mounted on the front of the torque tube, cooling by vaned flywheel, and (initially) two-wheel drum brakes. The engine's dimensions of 76.2mm bores and 101.6mm stroke displaced 1852cc, sufficient to propel the car at 50mph and return 23mpg on test. The chassis used a wheelbase of 9'3" and had an overall length of 12'6" – adequate to carry comfortable passenger coachwork.

The suspension of the first cars departed from established practice by using quarter elliptic springs all round, without shock absorbers,

and actuation of the brakes by cables; both handbrake and footbrake operated the two sets of shoes in the rear drums, and wheels were steel discs shod with 30 X 3½" high pressure tyres, or optionally with 4.25 X 31 balloon tyres.

Consistent with the company's policy of continual development, the car was in 1924 fitted with a scuttle-mounted fuel gauge, and 4.95 X 29 balloon tyres were optionally available. An open tourer weighed just over one ton, which allowed a sprightly performance in this form. Despite problems of high-speed instability caused by the unusual springing, the car was highly regarded and around 3000 were sold in its first two years of production. It was promoted as "A full sized touring car for family use at a price which makes it a better investment than any imported product".

From June, 1925, a Mark II version was available, differing in some significant respects from its predecessor. A new chassis with wheelbase of 9'6" was sprung by semi-elliptic springs instead of the original quarter elliptics, with four-wheel brakes operated by rods rather than cables. Disc wheels wore 4.95 X 29 balloon tyres, and 5.25 X 30 covers were optionally available for heavier loads.

Engine and transmission were identical to the original, but thanks to better brakes and less wayward handling the new series was noted for its unstressed point-to-point touring ability. The majority of bodies were built in-house by Burlington, and included limousines, landaulettes and enclosed landaulettes in addition to more family-orientated saloons, tourers and 2-seaters. Notable outsiders to apply their craft to the Fourteen included Connaught Motor & Carriage Co, Coventry Hood & Body Company, Fountain's Coach & Motor Co Ltd, Maltby's Motor Works and H J Mulliner. Production peaked in 1926, after which sales tailed off toward 1929 when the lower end of the Siddeley range became crowded following release of the Fifteen and the Twelve.

Contemporary opinions expressed by owners were quoted in company handouts, and included the following: "Since I took delivery of your 14hp car it has exceeded my expectation in the smoothness of running and the power it possesses among the hills: in fact, it is the hills where it shows itself to advantage. In my seventeen years' motoring I have not experienced its equal" and: "The car has created a very great impression, and when she was tackling a strenuous hill near Hayton, Dartmoor, was greeted with many cries of appreciation from other motorists." Now honestly, when was the last time fellow motorists applauded your Toyota's hill-climbing performance? "I am very pleased indeed with the car you have supplied. I think it is a most excellent car for family purposes. The engine in particular has struck me by its silence and sweetness".

In Australia the motor industry was learning the promotional value of long-distance trials over the appalling roads which prevailed in that country in the 1920s. It is no surprise that the All British Motor House in Melbourne made the most of the performance by a Fourteen tourer in the Royal Automobile Club of Queensland Reliability Trial of 1926, which it won outright and was first in the fuel consumption test.

The final word on the 14hp came from aviator Mr (later Sir) Alan Cobham, who established records for return flights from London to Cape Town and London to Melbourne, in an aircraft powered by an Armstrong Siddeley 'Jaguar' radial engine. Writing of the Fourteen in August, 1926, he said: "... I have driven one myself for over fifteen months, covering about 14,000 miles, during which time it has only been filled up with oil, petrol and water, and is running now better than the day I bought it... I am a very hard user with a car, and on some big new roads in England, have averaged 45 to 48 miles an hour, over considerable periods. As you know, this means something far greater on the speedometer".

Late in the 1920s public preference favoured small six-cylinder side valve engines. Side valves were more easily repaired and serviced by the modest mechanical skills available beyond major cities; engines having six cylinders were believed to be smoother-running than fours, and carried some cachet of status. Into the late series Fourteen chassis was installed a side valve six of 1900cc, with 63.5mm bores and 101mm stroke, designated the 15hp. Crankshaft and camshaft ran in four white-metal bearings, and the flywheel fan was retained, as was magneto ignition and a Claudel Hobson carburettor fed by gravity from a scuttle-mounted tank. As before the engine drove through a single plate clutch to a three-speed crash gearbox mounted to the front

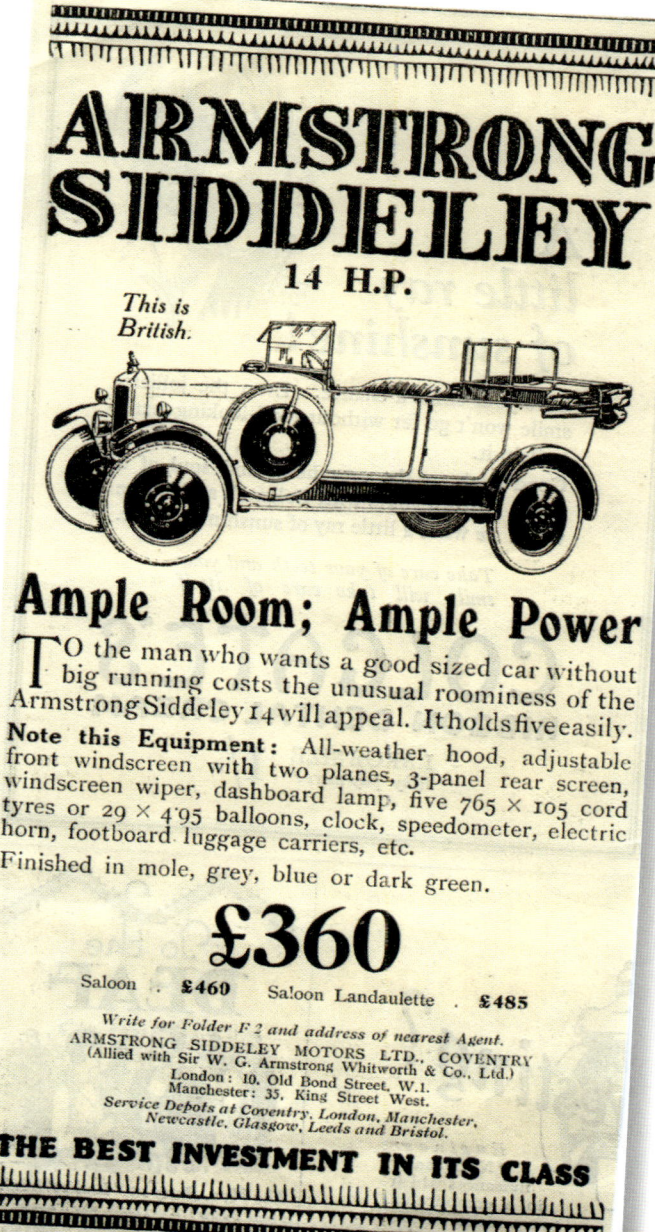

ARMSTRONG SIDDELEY 14 H.P.

This is British.

Ample Room; Ample Power

To the man who wants a good sized car without big running costs the unusual roominess of the Armstrong Siddeley 14 will appeal. It holds five easily.

Note this Equipment: All-weather hood, adjustable front windscreen with two planes, 3-panel rear screen, windscreen wiper, dashboard lamp, five 765 × 105 cord tyres or 29 × 4·95 balloons, clock, speedometer, electric horn, footboard, luggage carriers, etc.

Finished in mole, grey, blue or dark green.

£360

Saloon . £460   Saloon Landaulette . £485

Write for Folder F 2 and address of nearest Agent.
ARMSTRONG SIDDELEY MOTORS LTD., COVENTRY
(Allied with Sir W. G. Armstrong Whitworth & Co., Ltd.)
London : 10. Old Bond Street, W.1.
Manchester : 35. King Street West.
Service Depots at Coventry, London, Manchester, Newcastle, Glasgow, Leeds and Bristol.

THE BEST INVESTMENT IN ITS CLASS

The sub-units, fillers and filters are easily accessible.

The carburetter side of the engine shows its clean design.

Top: Offside of the Fourteen's overhead valve four-cylinder monobloc engine.

Above: Nearside of the engine, showing the updraught carburettor with exhaust-heated inlet tract.

end of the torque tube, and there were rod-operated four-wheel brakes. As for the late 4-14hp cars, there were gaitered semi-elliptic springs and steel disc wheels, shod with 4.95 X 29 or optionally 5.25 X 30 balloon tyres. The chassis was lubricated by a Tecalemit centralised system, which was applied to all models in the range except the Twelve from 1928.

Initially unchanged, its chassis in April, 1928, became underslung at the rear, and in February, 1929, a modified engine was introduced, and Luvax shock absorbers were fitted at the rear. From October, 1930, the frame was lowered and the flat radiator was replaced with a vee-fronted chromium-plated item similar to those on the larger cars. The big news in that year was fitment of a four-speed version of the preselector gearbox for an extra £40, allowing better use of the engine's modest output. At that time an alternative wheelbase length of 9'7" was introduced, dividing Fifteen production into the Long 15 and Short 15, the shorter of which rode at first on a 9'1" wheelbase, later (from January, 1932) extended to 9'2".

Common to both was a fuel tank relocated to the rear of the chassis feeding the engine via a mechanical pump, while modifications to the engine's combustion chambers and inlet manifolding produced

marginally more power. Steering became worm and segment adjustable for wear, while wire wheels were options to the standard steel discs for an extra £5.

From 1931 the engine was fitted with a crankshaft damper to address the periodic vibration experienced at about 45mph in top, while in 1932 the radiator was fitted with thermostatically-controlled shutters as on the larger cars, and finally the engine was cooled by a front-mounted fan. The BTH magneto gave way to Lucas coil ignition, and permanently fitted DWS jacks were attached beneath the rear springs and the front axle.

From November 1932 engine size was increased to 2169cc following an increase in the stroke to 114mm, and the cylinder head was again redesigned for more power. Bendix semi-servo brakes were operated by cables, worm and nut steering was introduced, and an electric fuel gauge was fitted. The last cars used downdraught Claudel Hobson carburettors.

The Short 15 followed a broadly similar development curve. Although initially a three-speed preselector gearbox was offered as an extra-cost option to the standard 3-speed crash 'box, a preselector 'box with four speeds was available from 1930; at that time its track was reduced to 4'4" reflecting the smaller, lighter and more sporting coachwork usually worn by the shorter cars.

For the time when the Fourteen was offered alongside the Fifteen, factory coachwork for both models was similar, providing a wide range of body styles to suit most tastes. Some available colour schemes bordered on the adventurous, but from contemporary photographs most appear to have been painted in dark and sombre tones.

The last 15hp car was built in July, 1934, at which time the overhead valve 17hp engine was installed in the late 15hp frame. The lively new 17hp car modernised the mid-range Armstrong Siddeley offerings, and laid the groundwork for a new generation of six-cylinder cars.

Whatever retrospective criticism may be applied to the side-valve Fifteen, the motoring press were effusive in their praise for the new car. Reporting on a Short 15 coachbuilt saloon in their issue of March 21, 1930, *The Autocar* said: "The new car possesses a similar but improved engine to the previous model, but the chassis has been largely redesigned, there being an option between a normal three-speed gearbox and the excellent four-speed self-changing gear, as well as a new transmission and a rear axle of the 'banjo' steel casing type. The saloon coachwork is new and is notable for combining an harmonious appearance with plenty of interior room. Altogether the new car is an exceedingly attractive family vehicle, useful alike for steady touring without waste of time, and for comfortable town work".

As always the company was eager to quote owners' opinions in their sales catalogues. One testimonial referring to the Fifteen reads: "The Fifteen hp is a most fascinating car to drive and the feeling of security is most enjoyable. She cruises easily at 55mph. My wife's favourite cruising speed is 45mph and at this speed it seems effortless progression for the car and a positive dream lullaby for the occupants".

And perhaps by way of dispelling any lingering impression that the Fifteen was a plodder, Mrs T H Wisdom (who together with her husband was a successful rally and trials driver) wrote of her Short Fifteen: "It was the first time that I had driven a car with self-changing gear and I must say I found it very light and easy to handle. What impressed me most after this ease of control was the super cornering and wonderful stability of the car.

"The self-centreing steering and road holding capabilities of the car are almost up to racing standards. The self-change gear made our task very easy and definitely does not take the fun out of driving. We found the body most comfortable especially in the rear seat, and by keeping up a good average speed were able to enjoy substantial stops at all the controls. In several cases we arrived before the controls opened".

Above: First series 14hp open tourer, showing adequate passenger accommodation.

ALL BRITISH MOTOR Co Pty Ltd
Russell Street Melbourne
Distributors of Britains Choicest Cars

ROLLS-ROYCE
The Best Car in the World

SUNBEAM
The Fastest Car in the World

ARMSTRONG-SIDDELEY
Britains Wonder Car

14/30 H.P. 4 CYL.
ARMSTRONG SIDDELEY COUPE

14/30 4 CYL. ARMSTRONG
SIDDELEY DE LUXE ROADSTER
(with dickie seat)

14/30 4 CYL. STANDARD
ARMSTRONG SIDDELY TOURER

14/30 4 CYL. ARMSTRONG
SIDDELEY DE LUXE TOURER

18/50 H.P. 6 CYL.
ARMSTRONG SIDDELEY STANDARD
TOURER

18/50 H.P. 6 CYL.
ARMSTRONG SIDDELEY

18/50 H.P. 6 CYL. DE LUXE
ARMSTRONG SIDDELEY TOURER

16 H.P. 6 CYL. DE LUXE
SUNBEAM TOURER

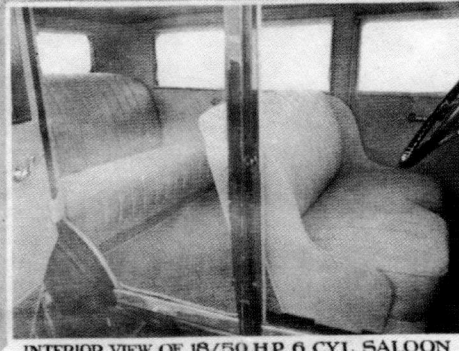

INTERIOR VIEW OF 18/50 H.P. 6 CYL. SALOON
ARMSTRONG SIDDELEY

14/30 H.P. 4 CYL.
ARMSTRONG SIDDELEY SALOON

20 H.P. 6 CYL.
ROLLS ROYCE SALOON

16 H.P. 6 CYL.
SUNBEAM SALOON

20 H.P. ROLLS ROYCE
DE LUXE TOURER

ALL THE ABOVE MODELS ARE FITTED WITH BODIES
MADE BY
MELBOURNE MOTOR BODY & ASSEMBLING CO. PTY. LTD.
DUDLEY ST. WEST MELBOURNE.

This 1927 advertisement by the All British Motor Company confirms that Australian-built coachwork was available on imported Armstrong Siddeley chassis.

THE ARMSTRONG SIDDELEY WORKS

THE thirty-two acre works at Coventry where the magnificent range of Armstrong Siddeley cars with the only proved self-changing gear are made side by side with the world-famous Siddeley air-cooled aero engines.

The company was suitably proud of its works in Coventry, and included this image in early sales brochures.

Right: Open tourer on the
2-wheel braked chassis.

Below right: 14hp Special
Equipment Model – note
the Auster screen for the rear
passengers.

Left: Two-seater Mark I 14hp with dickey seat.

Left below: 14hp saloon, probably built by Burlington.

Right: 14hp landaulette on the first series chassis.

Below: 14hp Mark II Mendip 2/3 seater, used by the Canberra, Australia, fire chief, here seen with his chauffeur at the wheel. National Australia Archive photo.

Below right: A privately owned Mark II 14hp tourer outside the partially completed Australian Parliament House building in 1929. National Australia Archive photo.

Sir Alan Cobham used
an Armstrong Siddeley Engine

LONDON——CAPETOWN——LONDON
ENGLAND——AUSTRALIA——ENGLAND
44,000 miles on one engine

ARMSTRONG · SIDDELEY · CARS

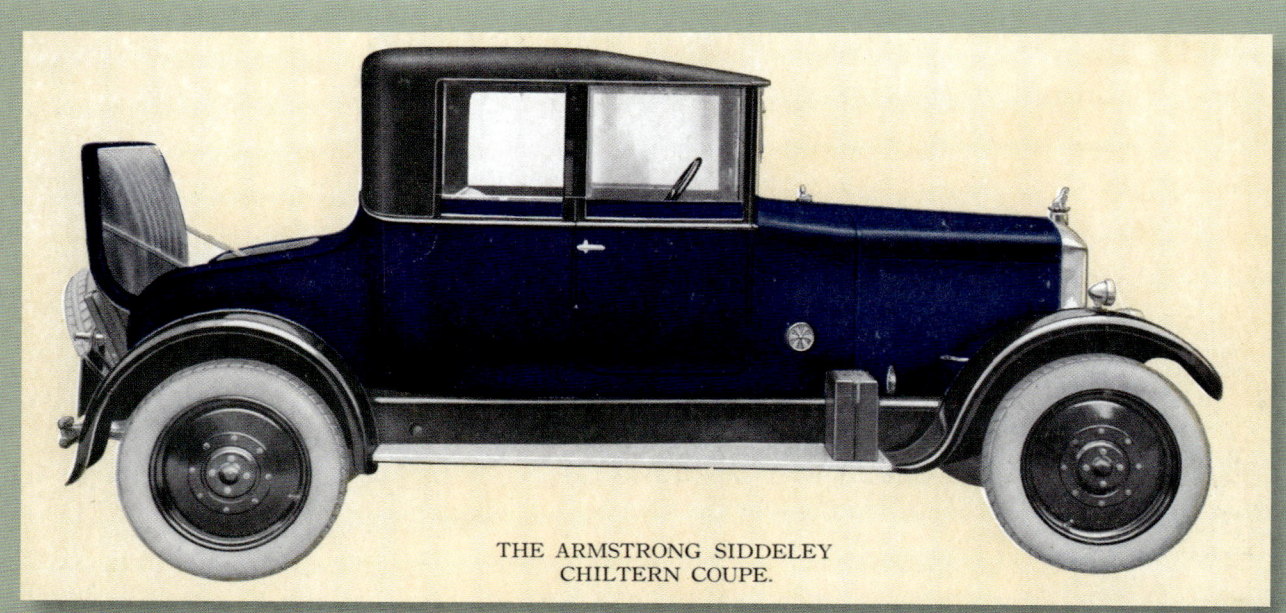

THE ARMSTRONG SIDDELEY
CHILTERN COUPE.

Above: Mark II 14hp Chiltern coupé.

Right: Handsome vee-windscreen on the Sandown Special Tourer.

THE ARMSTRONG SIDDELEY
SANDOWN SPECIAL TOURER
with the rigid and rattle-proof side panels
in position.

THE ARMSTRONG SIDDELEY
MENDIP TWO-THREE SEATER.

THE ARMSTRONG SIDDELEY
COTSWOLD FIVE SEATER TOURER.

Above: Mendip 2/3 seater roadster.

Left: The Cotswold 5-seater open tourer with full weather equipment.

85

THE ARMSTRONG SIDDELEY
BROADWAY SALOON.

Above: The 5-seater Broadway saloon.

Right: The Lynton Saloon-Landaulette on the late 14hp chassis.

THE ARMSTRONG SIDDELEY
LYNTON SALOON LANDAULETTE.

THE ARMSTRONG SIDDELEY
GRASMERE THREE-QUARTER
LANDAULETTE

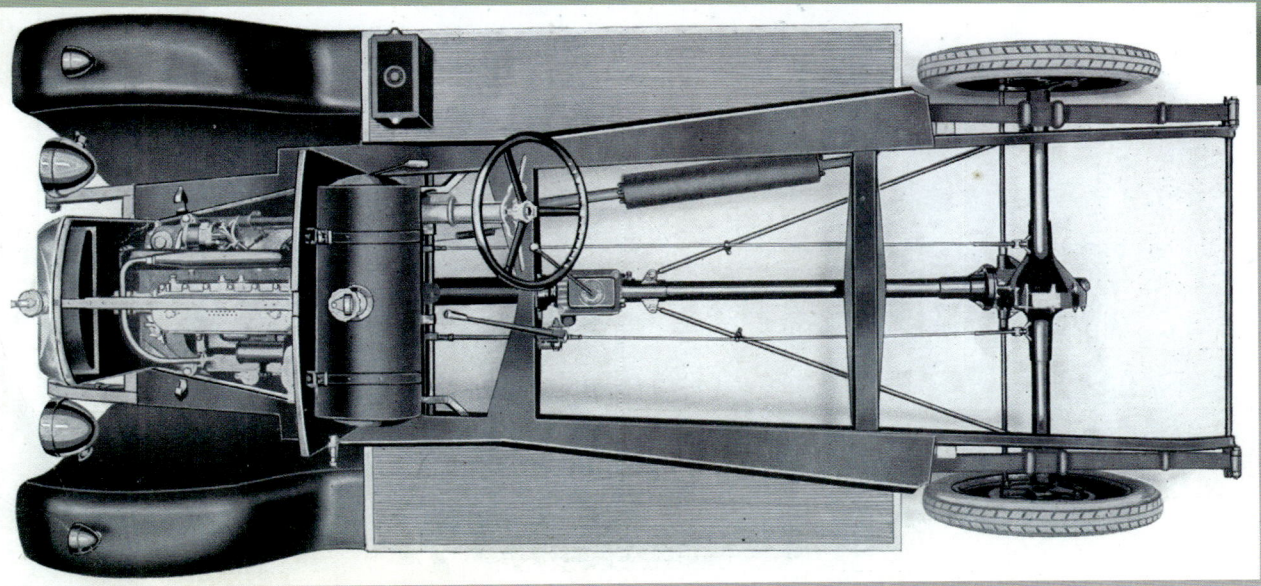

Above: The Grasmere Three-Quarter Landaulette - pretension on a budget.

Left: The 14hp Mark II chassis. Note the triangulated bracing to the rear axle, and the torque tube drive. The semi-elliptic springs of the later cars can also be clearly seen.

Above: The Mendip 2/3 seater
dickey-seat roadster

Right: The Cotswold tourer.

Above: The Broadway saloon.

Left: The Sandown Special tourer.

Above: The Manston fabric saloon.

Right: The Lonsdale Saloon.

Above: The Grasmere Three-Quarter landaulette.

Left: The Lynton Saloon-Landaulette.

Above: Unusual "2/6 seater" Coachbuilt Saloon by Norvic Carriagework (Howes and Sons Ltd) of Norwich. Apparently a two-seat fixed head coupé, the makers' brochure says there were two extra occasional seats in the front, and space for two more in the dickey seat.

Right: The attractive Curzon fixed-head coupé was an addition to the range of 14hp coachwork for 1928, again available also on the 15hp chassis.

The first 15hp cars were almost indistinguishable from their 14hp stablemates. Illustrated in a first series 1928 open tourer.

Burlington coachbuilt saloon body on the Long 15 chassis, photographed as
part of a fuel bowser promotion, in Aberdeen, 1930.

The early flat-radiator 15hp was available as a Special tourer (above) or the standard tourer (below). There was some status attached to front-opening front doors.

Top: From 1930 the 15hp wore a Vee-fronted radiator similar to its larger siblings.
Here is the 1931 open tourer.
Above: Also from 1931 is this semi-panelled saloon, offered in fabric
or all-steel (lower right) bodywork.
Right top: This very attractive Sunshine Coupé body was available on the
15hp and the 20hp chassis.
Right centre: Burlington's coachbuilt saloon was a dependable favourite
as a commodious passenger car.

Left: The factory's commodious coachbuilt saloon on the Long chassis was current for 1934.

Bottom left: Hoyal (Chalmer & Hoyer, of Weybridge and Hamsworthy) built this stylish Deluxe Half-Panel Saloon on both the 15hp and 20hp chassis, charging an extra £15 for a sunroof, but the window draught-excluders were standard.

Bottom right: Hoyal also built this handsome coachbuilt saloon.

Upper left: The last 15hp cars were known as 15/40hp. Shown here is the attractive Short roadster complete with optional bolt-on wire wheels.

Left: Here is the 15/40 Coachbuilt Saloon by Burlington, the last of the line.

Above: This 1934 15hp Sportsmans Saloon was complete with a sunshine roof.

The 15 h.p. Sports Saloon
£388

Here is a medium weight, medium powered car with a really good performance

THE Fifteen h.p. Sports Saloon is a fast car that is comfortable to drive, economical to run and easy to maintain. Its body is of the type that did so well in last year's Elegance Competitions and incorporates such special Armstrong Siddeley features as the hidden luggage grid and container, lever-free front compartment, wide angle driving view and seats of armchair comfort.

May we send you our Catalogue?

Armstrong Siddeley Motors Ltd., Coventry.   London: 10 Old Bond St., W.1.   Manchester: 35 King St. West

BP232A

Right: Quantities of complete chassis were shipped to Sydney, Australia. Armstrong Siddeley dealers, Buckle Motors, commissioned locally-made coachwork to save payment of Government duties applicable to complete cars. This 1933 15hp wears a saloon body of unknown parentage, but possibly by Ruskin of Melbourne.

Below: Handsome Sports Saloon on the 1933 15hp chassis, probably by Burlington, and similar to the same body on the 20hp chassis.

Burlington built this attractive Sports Saloon on the 1934 15hp Short chassis. Note that the occupants appear microcephalic in the interests of making the car's interior look cavernous.

Factory designation	14hp	14hp Mark II
Date introduced	July 1923	June 1925
Motor type	4-cyl 4-stroke water-cooled monobloc ohv	same
Dimensions	76.2 X 101.6mm = 1853cc	same
Power/rpm	14.4hp RAC rating	same
Fuel feed	gravity feed to single Claudel Hobson carb	same
Ignition	BTH magneto	same
Transmission type	3-spd & rev crash gearbox, central lever	same
Ratios	17.5 8.63 4.7:1 Rev 22.25:1	same
Final drive ratio	4.7:1 spiral bevel drive	same
Clutch	single dry plate	same
Steering		
Suspension		
Front	quarter-elliptic springs	gaitered semi-elliptic springs
Rear	quarter-elliptic springs	gaitered semi-elliptic springs
Brakes	2-whl drum brakes on rear only, rod operated	4-whl drum brakes, rod operated
Wheels	detachable steel discs	same
Tyres	4.95 X 29" or 765 X 105mm optional	same, Dunlop 5.25 X 30" optional
Dimensions		
Wheelbase	9'3"	9'6"
Track front	4'3"	same
Track rear	4'8"	same
Overall length	12'6"	13'2"
Overall width	5'6"	same
Height	dependent on body style & coachbuilder	tourer 6'3" hood erect, saloon similar, landaulette 6'4"
Unladen weight		
Factory coachwork	tourer, 2/3 seater roadster, saloon	Cotswold tourer, Sandown Special tourer, Chiltern coupé, Mendip 2/3 seater, Broadway saloon, Curzon coupé, Manston fabric saloon, Lynton saloon landaulette, Grasmere ¾ landaulette
Variants	per outside coachbuilders	same
Performance		
Max speed (mph)	55	same
Fuel consumption (mpg)	26-28	same
Number produced	3076	11,479
Prices	tourer £400	Chassis £230, tourer £325, special tourer £360, coupé £425, 2/3 str £325, saloon £375, landaulette £425
Date last produced	May 1925	May 1929

Factory designation	15hp	Long 15hp & Short 15hp
Date introduced	October 1927	(Long) Oct 1930 (Short) Dec 1930
Motor type	6-cyl 4-stroke in-line water-cooled side valves	same
Dimensions	63.5 X 101mm = 1900cc (1929 revised engine)	Nov 1932 – stroke 114mm = 2169cc
Power/rpm	15hp RAC rating	
Fuel feed	gravity feed to single Claudel Hobson updraught carb (1932 – Claudel Hobson V36 AD2)	rear tank, (Dec 1933 downdraught CH carb)
Ignition	BTH magneto	Nov 1932, battery & coil ignition
Transmission type	3-spd & rev crash gearbox (4-spd Wilson 'box from March 1930)	same
Ratios	19 9.35 5:1 Rev 24:1 (20.5 10 5.5 from April 1928)	(Short) 19 11 7.4 5.1 (Long) 21.2 12.1 7.8 5.3:1
Final drive ratio	5:1 torque tube drive to spiral bevel axle (5.5:1 from April 1928)	(Short) 5.1:1 (Long) 5.3:1
Clutch	single dry plate for crash 'box	none, Wilson 'box
Steering	worm& segment, adjustable for rake	1932 – worm & nut mechanism
Suspension		
Front	gaitered semi-elliptic springs (+ Luvax dampers from July 1929)	same
Rear	gaitered semi-elliptic springs (+Luvax dampers from July 1929)	same
Brakes	4-whl drums rod operated	same
Wheels	detachable steel discs	same, bolt-on wires optional + £5
Tyres	4.95 X 29 or 5.25 X 30 optional (5.00 X 30 from April 1928)	5.00 X 19"
Dimensions		
Wheelbase	9'6"	(short) 9'1" (long) 9'7"
Track front	4'8"	4'8" (both)
Track rear	4'8"	4'8" (both)
Overall length	13'7"-13'9" depending on coachwork	(short) 12'7" (long) 13'1"
Overall width	5'8"	same (both)
Height	5'7" – 6'3" depending on coachwork	same
Factory coachwork	fabric saloons (4/6 lt), coachbuilt saloon, tourer, Weymann saloon	(short) Weymann & metal 4-lt saloons, tourer (long) Weymann saloon, semi-panelled saloon
Variants	per outside coachbuilders	same
Performance		
Max speed (mph)	60	65
Fuel consumption (mpg)	24	23-24
Number produced	4864 (to Oct 1930)	(short) 1504 (long) 3100
Prices	fabric saloons & tourer £360 coachbuilt & Weymann saloons £395	chass £260 tourer £350 Weymann 4-lt saloon £365 metal 4-lt saloon £380
Date last produced	September 1930	(short) July 1934 (long) September 1934

CHAPTER V

THE 12, 12 PLUS + 14HP
1928-1939

Siddeley learned from Herbert Austin's Seven that the market preferred a scaled-down full-sized car to a scaled-up cyclecar. He proved with his Fifteen that modestly-sized cars powered by a six-cylinder engine had specific appeal, and resolved to downsize even further into small car territory. The outcome was the 1236cc Twelve unveiled at the October, 1928 Olympia Motor Show.

Although the Twelve is often described as the first of the small sixes, the 1923 British BSA was driven by six cylinders of just 1028cc. The French Amilcar C6 used a six of just 1089cc in supercharged and dual overhead camshaft form in 1926, and the German Rosengart six displaced just 1097cc. Some most enterprising small sixes included the overhead valve 1612cc Talbot 12/30 of 1924, and in 1927 the 1860cc overhead camshaft Calthorpe and the 1477cc AC also with upstairs camshaft.

What distinguished Armstrong Siddeley's Twelve was its inclusion of most if not all of the creature comforts of its larger stablemates. In all ways it resembled a scaled-down Fifteen – from its side-valve six cylinder engine, through its three-speed crash gearbox attached to the forward end of the torque tube, four wheel rod-operated brakes, steel disc wheels, flywheel fan, flat-fronted radiator, chain-driven dynamo and magneto, gravity-feed fuel supply to a Claudel Hobson carburettor, and semi-elliptic springing.

The Twelve, perhaps more than any other model embodied the Armstrong Siddeley philosophy of building motorcars. The first saloons were lounges on wheels, their propelling units almost incidental to the passengers' needs to travel from one place to another in unruffled comfort, their drawing rooms not far removed in style from the cars' beautifully appointed interiors.

Lampooned by some latter-day motoring writers as underpowered, the Twelve must be placed in its market context. Even the first cars would exceed 50mph and cruise at 40mph, not long after larger-engined bread-and-butter family saloons struggled to reach 40mph at all; recall that the 2.8 litre Ford Model T was built until 1927, yet only a brave or foolish man would try to drive one at 50mph.

Early coachwork was typically a fabric-clad saloon of Weymann appearance, the car weighing less than a ton. Reflecting manufacturing pressures created by their Twelve, Fifteen, Twenty and Thirty horsepower cars, the factory sub-contracted construction of the bodies for most of the first series saloons to Holbrook Bodies of Coventry – a minor player in the coachbuilding industry which relied on work building Standards. Holbrooks also built a two-seater roadster, while a fixed-head coupé was added by the Hoyal Body Corporation of Weybridge in Surrey.

The Motor of October 2, 1928 enthused: "All the detail work in both engine and chassis has had just as much care and attention bestowed upon it as the larger models, while workmanship and finish are quite up to the same high standard as is reached by all the company's more expensive products."

The Autocar welcomed the new model in its issue of October 5, 1928: "...the new 12hp Armstrong Siddeley car follows the customary style of design adopted by its makers, in that sturdiness is the feature which is intended to stand out in the construction of the chassis, and to this point other considerations are more or less subservient".

Introduction of the heavier Burlington coachbuilt saloon late in 1929 tested the engine's power, so in October, 1930 capacity was lifted to 1434cc after Mr (later Sir) Harry Ricardo recommended a significant redesign. The Mark II Twelve incorporated the high-swirl cylinder head designed by Ricardo for a number of contemporary side-valve engines. Additionally the season's cars were fitted with Luvax shock-absorbers and a three-speed preselector gearbox, ignition was changed from magneto to Lucas coil with automatic advance and retard mechanism, the rear axle was strengthened in response to heavier weights, and Silentbloc bushes were fitted to all spring shackles.

Factory coachwork included a 'Sunshine Saloon', a fabric-covered four door four-seater whose equipment included a sliding roof, an extended luggage compartment and fitted luggage. Testing the larger-engined Sunshine Saloon on February 10, 1931, *The Motor* said: "The Armstrong Siddeley Twelve is a very 'nippy' car in traffic, for steering, brakes and engine response are of a high order, while the preselector mechanism allows one to concentrate on steering... With the speedometer needle hovering near the 50mph mark the power unit is not at all obtrusive..." In the same year *Light Car & Cyclecar*

Above: First series Twelve open tourer 1929.

magazine listed speeds in gears as 15, 27, 40 and 60mph, which compared more than favourably with even the larger-engined Austins and Morrises of the time.

In late 1931, the Twelve range divided into the Deluxe and the Economy models, the principal differences being the employment of a four-speed preselector transmission and a Vee-shaped radiator for the Deluxe; the fuel tank was relocated to the back of the car and fed the engine via a mechanical fuel pump on both versions. The track was also widened by two inches, and a crankshaft damper was fitted to overcome a periodic vibration at around 38mph in top gear.

From October, 1932 the Economy range was fitted with a shallow Vee-shaped radiator cowl, and on all models the vaned flywheel finally gave way to a belt-driven fan at the front of the motor, new Bendix semi-servo brakes were cable-operated, DWS permanently fitted jacks were installed front and rear as on the larger models, and a Lucas Startix was fitted (the Startix enabled one touch to operate the starter

until the engine fired). Bolt-on wire wheels were options to the steel discs for an extra £5, while a sunroof cost an additional £10.

Coachbuilders produced some handsome bodywork on the Twelve as well as the standard range, including an all-weather saloon and coupé-cabriolet from Tickford, a drophead coupé and 'Style' foursome saloon by Maltby, and a sports coupé, foursome coupé and coupé-cabriolet from Charlesworth.

Perhaps inspired by Maltby's foursome saloon, or their own 'Foursome' on their new 17hp chassis, Armstrong Siddeley gilded the lily by introducing the 12hp coupé in October, 1933. Built on a new frame with shorter wheelbase and narrower track, the coupé was a two-door four-seater with very smart lines and less weight than the four-door saloons. Still using the 1434cc side-valve engine with four-speed preselector transmission, the car was tested at 65mph and returned better than 25mpg. With the spin long associated with factory publicist W G McMinnies, it was promoted as being ideal "for the daughters of gentlemen". Apparently paupers need not apply.

The Motor tested a coupé and reported in its issue of October 30, 1934: "For long runs 50mph is a pleasant cruising speed, although well over 60mph can be attained with ease, and in spite of its refined and dignified appearance it is a 'go-anywhere' car". On test their car recorded a maximum speed of 62.5mph, with 46mph available on third and 29mph on second. These figures are very close to performance figures for the much-lauded 1949 Morris Minor, which could not offer anything like the style, space and comfort of the Twelve coupe built 17 years earlier.

The coupé was last sold in October, 1936. It was a thoroughly modern design which, together with the new Seventeen, rattled the image of Armstrong Siddeleys as hyper-conservative and matronly cars. But the best was yet to come.

Encouraged by the early market success of this car, in early 1934 Amstrong Siddeley built three aluminium-bodied prototype sports tourers, complete with wire wheels and cutaway doors in the manner of the contemporary MG Midgets. These most handsome cars were

entered in that year's RAC Rally, and subsequently steel-bodied examples were catalogued and 250 were produced.

From late 1935, the Twelve became the Twelve Plus, with installation into a strengthened frame of a new 1666cc engine with overhead valves. The Newton centrifugal clutch was standard wear in association with the four-speed preselector gearbox, both fan and dynamo were belt-driven, and fuel feed was via a side-draught Claudel Hobson carburettor and mechanical pump. Even in saloon form the new car could comfortably exceed 65mph. There was a new Deluxe saloon and a very smart four-door four-light sports saloon, which took its styling cues from the successful coupé. Using a central pillar from which swung front and rear doors, an ingenious mechanism ensured that the semaphore-type trafficators then installed would not be damaged should both doors be opened at once.

Below: Burlington-built 2-3 seater roadster.

Opposite page: 1928 fabric saloon, built by Holbrooks.

The motoring press continued to be impressed with the evolving model, *The Motor* publishing its impressions of the Deluxe 6-light saloon on March 3, 1936: "Refinement is an outstanding characteristic, the engine and transmission being smooth and quiet, while the controls are responsive and call for a minimum of physical effort... The overhead valve engine, although so quiet and smooth, develops exceptional torque and power and consequently gets away with its load in an easy and convincing manner".

In the following year, the model name was changed to the Fourteen, and the rear track was increased. In October, 1937 the advent of 'Balanced Drive' dispensed with the use of the jack-shaft between the engine and the gearbox, connecting both units for the first time. The rear springs were underslung and mounted outboard of the frame. On test the new 14hp saloon reached 50mph from rest in 22 seconds and comfortably topped 65mph. *Practical Motorist* summed up the range of Armstrong Siddeley models in their issue of September 5, 1936: "The cars are moderately priced and offer outstanding value amongst the high-grade motor cars of to-day. Furthermore, their improved performance, and their stylish coachwork, typified by the new 'Atalanta' saloon, place them in the first rank of modern quality cars".

During its production run the Twelve grew from a model which was clearly on the bottom rung of the Armstrong Siddeley range, to one which created its own market sector. In final form its performance equalled that of well-regarded sporting cars like the 1½ litre Riley, and bettered that of its quality contemporaries like Wolseley and Triumph. Factory coachwork comprised designs ranging from the ultra-restrained to the stylish and sporting, prompting one Australian agent to promote the Twelve as the 'Lynx' and the Fourteen as the 'Panther' – complete with suitable hyperbole connecting the cars with the company's aero engines. The termination of the Fourteen in 1938 recognised that its market sector was becoming crowded with able competitors, while the move upmarket with the new Sixteen heralded the more limited model range which would follow.

Top right and below: Burlington coachbuilt steel-panelled saloon. The extra weight caused a rethink on the engine's power output.

Above: Sportmans Coupé built by Norvic Carriageworks, Norwich.

Far left Burlington's fabric-clad Sunshine Saloon of 1930.

Left: Shapely tail of the Sunshine Saloon concealed a useful luggage compartment.

Above: The cabin of the Sunshine Saloon was well-furnished, with leather, carpet and deep door pockets.

Above right: The luggage compartment of the Sunshine Saloon was supplied with fitted luggage to maximise its usefulness, and the ease with which it could be loaded by lady drivers.

Right: Sydney doctor C Eden George believed the hype that the 12 coupé was suitable 'for the daughters of gentlemen', and in 1934 bought his daughter this fine example as a stablemate for his New 20.

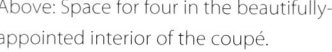

Above: Space for four in the beautifully-appointed interior of the coupé.

Above and top right: From the side and the tail the coupé was always stylish and modern.

Top left: The 12 coupé was built on a smaller chassis and was very well-received as a handsome and nippy small car.

Above: The coupé offered useful stowage despite its truncated tail.

Left: The coupé came standard with a four-speed Wilson gearbox and Bluemels sprung steering wheel.

This page: Adventurous colour schemes ensured that the coupé was always noticed.

Opposite page: Sydney coachbuilder Creswell built this modern and sporty four door saloon, on commission from Buckle Motors.

Left: Twelve chassis as used by Sydney's Buckle Motors to ferry their cars to local coachbuilders.

Opposite page: Creswell bodied Twelve in company with an aircraft at Sydney's Double Bay.

Above: Buckle Motors commissioned Ruskin of Melbourne to build this six-light saloon body for their 1932 Twelve.

Right: Handsome four-door open tourer, Australian bodied, possibly by Ruskin of Melbourne for Buckle Motors of Sydney.

Top right: Ruskin-bodied six-light Twelve saloon in Australian location.

Perpetuating the company's attachment to high profile airmen, this photo shows Sir Charles Kingsford-Smith
with a Ruskin-bodied Twelve, probably supplied for his use for promotional purposes.

Right: Ruskin-bodied six-light Twelve saloon commissioned by Buckle Motors of Sydney.

Opposite page: Post-1932 Burlington coachbuilt saloon with Vee-radiator.

Coachbuilt DeLuxe Saloon on the early 1930s Twelve.

Twelve Economy saloon from the same era. Note that it retained the flatter radiator shell.

Above: Tickford landaulette, hood erect, on the Twelve chassis.

Right: The Tickford landaulette with hood lowered.

Above right: The overhead valve 1666cc engine powered what was first known as the Twelve Plus, and then as the Fourteen, to the end of the model's life in 1939.

Below: First to utilise the ohv engine was the six-light Burlington-built saloon.

Bottom: 250 of these handsome steel-bodied open tourers were built by Burlington, following the good reception of three prototypes constructed of alloy.

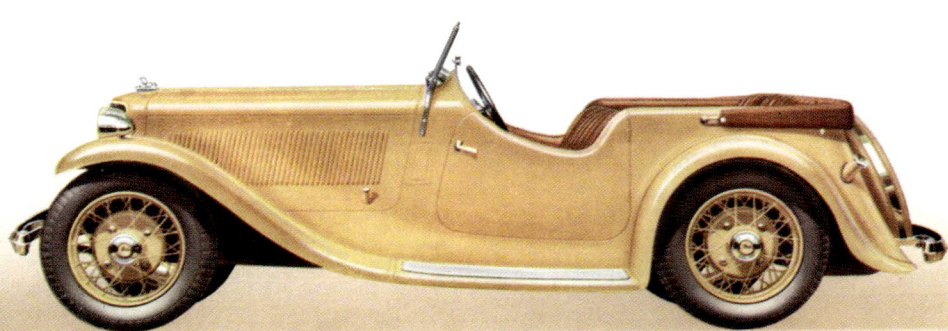

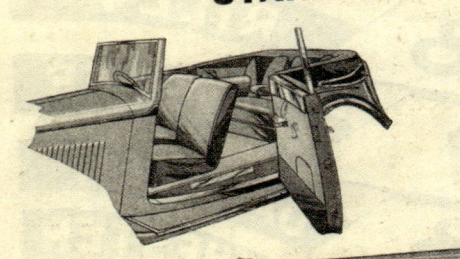
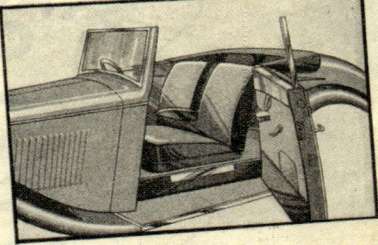
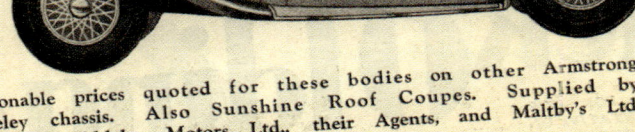

THE 14 H.P. FOUR-LIGHT SALOON.

This is a light four door, compact car of pleasing and fashionable lines with a very satisfying performance. Graceful lines have been attained without the restriction of passenger comfort. Plenty of head, leg and arm room is provided in both front and rear seats **£320**

COLOURS: BLUE, GREEN, GREY & BLACK

Right: The four light sports saloon followed the styling leads of the successful coupé, offering more space.

Above: Twelve Plus coachbuilt saloon, with overhead valve engine.

Right: This advertisement for Melbourne dealer Stokoe Motors gives prices in Australian pounds. Note the locally-bodied Ruskin alternatives for each model in the range.

Price List

(Effective from 7th May, 1937)

ARMSTRONG-SIDDELEY

British Cars of Aircraft Quality.

14 h.p. MODELS, 108 in. wheelbase.

Ruskin De Luxe Saloon	£495
Imported Sports Saloon . . .	£595
Imported County Saloon . .	£595

17 h.p. MODELS, 116 in. wheelbase.

Ruskin De Luxe Saloon	£745
Imported Touring Saloon . .	£845
Imported "Atalanta" Saloon	£925

25 h.p. MODELS, 131 in. wheelbase.

Ruskin De Luxe Saloon	£975
Martin & King De Luxe Saloon	£1095
Imported Touring Saloon . .	£1075
Imported "Atalanta" Saloon	£1150

All prices and specifications are subject to change without notice.

Exclusive distributors, Victoria and Riverina

STOKOE MOTORS PTY. LTD.

265-273 Exhibition Street, Melbourne, C.I., - - F4181

125

The Panth Model
ARMSTRONG-SIDDELEY
Sports Saloon.

Right: Melbourne, Australia's Clemenger Motors marketed the Fourteen as the Panther, the Twelve as the Lynx, and the New 20 as the Jaguar – attaching all models to aero engines manufactured by Armstrong Siddeley. After World War 2, the factory followed their lead, but by then Sir John Siddeley had given Sir William Lyons permission to use the Jaguar name, and the rest is history.

Opposite page: Heavy saloon body by Ruskin of Melbourne on a Fourteen echoes the strongly American style of many of the Ruskin company's products.

The **Armstrong-Siddeley Panther** 6-cylinder Model

ECONOMY WITH QUALITY

All Armstrong-Siddeley cars are built to the same aircraft standards of quality, and the Panther model is a finely finished, sturdily built, dependable and enduring car. On account of its size and weight it is very economical to run and easy to drive.

Named after the world-famous Armstrong-Siddeley Aero Engines, the Panther model is backed by five years' experience in the hands of the public and is acknowledged to represent the best combination of qualities that are desirable in a car of this class.

It is essentially the light car de luxe. With its four-speed gear and smooth six-cylinder engine driving possesses new pleasures. An intense feeling of safety and certainty is induced by the self-changing gear and its steering wheel control, so that gear changing actually becomes a joy instead of an anxiety.

Those who lay store by performance will be amazed at the perfect ease with which high average speeds can be maintained.

This performance is combined with the enduring economy of running which has always characterised Armstrong-Siddeley cars. Their aircraft quality is reflected in their utter dependability over long periods. Freedom from trouble, however hard or long the journey, is the key-note to the success of the Panther. Thus to extreme ease of driving it adds simplicity and cheapness of upkeep, and so makes a strong appeal to all.

THE COACHWORK

The coachwork reaches the same high standard of excellence. It is built to last and to maintain its lustre. Extremely modern in appearance, its handsome lines have been attained without going to extremes which may produce a cramped, uncomfortable position, bad ventilation, or lack of accommodation. All the bodies are hand-built of Queensland Maple, English Steel, upholstered in real leather, and lacquered any colour to choice.

The Armstrong-Siddeley Panther is the kind of car that people of discrimination appreciate. It looks good, it's made well and it's comfortable.

SOLE DISTRIBUTORS FOR VICTORIA:

Clemenger Motors Pty. Limited

128-30 RUSSELL STREET — MELBOURNE. C.1.

Top: More handsome was the factory's six-light saloon, heralding a whole new body style for the range.

Right: The Touring Saloon body style, with prominent and angular luggage boot extension, was applied across the model range. However practical, the luggage boot spoiled otherwise handsome lines.

Opposite page: Australian six-light saloon commissioned by Buckle Motors, and possibly built by Properts of Sydney.

"The History of England is emphatically the History of Progress" 1835.

IT is with admiration tinged with envy that other nations of the world behold the inspiring progress of England. In all spheres of thought and action does she excel. The great things of the world she has conceived and planned and carried to fruition. In engineering endeavor, British craftsmanship has won the esteem of all nations. And it is this traditional faculty for understanding engineering principles that has enabled Britain to produce so fine a car as the Armstrong-Siddeley.

Built side by side with utterly dependable aeroplanes, this car of aircraft quality, performs with perfect precision, operates silently, efficiently, effortlessly. Its appearance, too, is marked with a degree of dignity that typifies the country from which it emanates. The Armstrong-Siddeley is indeed a fine car with a famous name—a car and a name that are appreciated by those who value the good things of life.

Fitted with the only proven self-changing gears
1935 MODELS NOW ON DISPLAY PRICED FROM
£425 to £1675

ARMSTRONG SIDDELEY

The Car of Aircraft Quality

CLEMENGER MOTORS PTY. LTD.
128 RUSSELL STREET, MELBOURNE. M 4400.

Melbourne, Australia Armstrong Siddeley dealer, Clemenger Motors, commissioned a number of locally-built bodies on imported chassis from companies like Ruskin, Martin & King and others. All were geared for producing clones of American bodies on makes like Chevrolet, Dodge and Packard, and this advertisement clearly shows the strong American influence on those they sold.

Factory designation	12hp	12hp Mark II	12 Plus/14hp
Date introduced	Olympia Motor Show, October 1928	Olympia Motor Show, October 1930	September 1935
Motor type	6-cyl 4-stroke water-cooled monobloc side valves	same	same but overhead valves
Dimensions	56 X 84mm = 1236cc	56.5 X 92.25mm = 1434cc	61 X 95.24mm = 1666cc
Power/rpm	11.6hp RAC rating	11.9hp RAC rating	
Fuel feed	gravity feed to single Claudel Hobson carburettor	same, Zenith carb on coupé & tourer	mech pump side-draught Claudel Hobson carb
Ignition	BTH magneto with automatic advance/retard	battery and coil	same
Transmission type	3-spd & Rev crash gearbox	same but 3-spd Wilson 'box optional +£25 or £30	all 4-spd & Rev Wilson
Ratios	16.8 8.85 5.1:1 Rev 23:1(first series)	(crash) 18.25 9.62 5.55:1 (Wilson) 19.64 11.5 5.77:1	19.2 11.15 7.55 5.33:1
	18.04 9.55 5.5:1 Rev 24.07:1 (sunshine saloon)	(Wilson coupé & tourer) 11.7 7.9 5.5:1 – Rev 20.25:1)	
Final drive ratio	5.5:1 spiral bevel drive	(crash) 5.55:1 (Wilson) 5.77:1	5.33:1
Clutch	single dry plate	same for crash gearbox version	Newton centrifugal
Steering	worm & nut	same	same
Suspension			
Front	gaitered semi-elliptic spings, Luvax dampers (1930+)	same	same
Rear	gaitered underslung semi-elliptic springs & dampers	same	same
Brakes	four wheel drum brakes rod operated		
Wheels	19" steel disc	same, wire wheels optional with Wilson 'box +£5	17" steel disc
Tyres	4.40 X 27 cross ply	same, 4.75 X 18" for coupé and tourer	5.00 X 17"
Dimensions			
Wheelbase	8'9"	same, 8'1" for sports coupé & tourer from Oct 1933	12+ dimensions same as previously (14hp) 9'0"
Track front	4'	4'2", 3'10" for coupé & tourer	4'2"
Track rear	4'	4'4", 3'10" for coupé & tourer	4'6"
Overall length	13'	12'10", 12'1" for coupé & tourer	13'8"
Overall width	5'1"	5'3", 4'10" for coupé & tourer	5'4"
Height	5'7½" (fabric saloon) 5'6" (tourer) 5'4" (2-str)	varied according to coachwork	same
Factory coachwork	fabric saloon tourer 2-str coach saloon Hoyal coupé	coachbuilt/sunshine/sports/Economy sports saloons open & 2-str tourers	6-lt saloon Touring saloon
Variants	per outside coachbuilders in UK and elsewhere	same, eg Charlesworth, Cresswell, Maltby, Ruskin etc	same, eg Maltby and Salmons
Performance			
Max speed (mph)	55	60	65 (12+ sports tourer)
Fuel consumption (mpg)	30mpg (Factory claim)		
Number produced	3250	7750	3750
Prices	chassis £175 (+ £25 for Wilson 'box)	Economy saloon £260 coachbuilt saloon £295	6-lt saloon £320 touring saloon £330
	2/3 str/tourer £250 Sunshine/coachbuilt saloons £270	sunshine saloon £300 2/3-str & tourer £285 (1932)	
Date last produced	October 1930	August 1935	December 1939

THE SIDDELEY SPECIAL MK I AND MK II
1933-1937

What price a legend? How should the contemporary market view a motor car costing £1000 in 1933 built alongside a side-valve 12hp car for £265? What could have convinced its makers that an opulent and costly limousine would find buyers in the midst of a world Depression?

The answer lies somewhere between the long gestation period of an extraordinary design, and the personal ambitions of its manufacturer. As early as 1927 and possibly earlier, Siddeley engaged Fred Allard, an engineer in the company's Development and Experimental division, to design a new top-of-the-line replacement for the ageing 30hp. Allard was instructed to take advantage of the company's experience in aircraft manufacture, and specifically to make use of research work by High Duty Alloys Limited – a company then controlled by Siddeley and later by Rolls-Royce.

Siddeley's interest in lightweight alloys possibly extended back to his importation of the Marmon car which he dismantled in 1918, since the Model 34 made extensive use of alloy in its mechanical components. For use primarily in aircraft, High Duty Alloys had developed 'Hiduminium', an aluminium alloy offering light weight,

great strength and heat-absorbing qualities ideal for a large motor car engine. The mighty 37.2hp Hispano Suiza launched in 1919 employed steel cylinder liners screwed into an alloy block, so the precedent existed, and what a precedent.

Displayed as a chassis at the 1932 Olympia Motor Show, the Special engine's architecture was in all ways massive, with bores of 88.9mm and stroke of 133.4mm displacing 4960cc – identical to the old Thirty. Initially fed by a single Claudel Hobson carburettor, fuel feed was early changed to two SUs, standardised in January, 1934. At the same time the original mechanical valve tappets were replaced by hydraulic actuation in the interests of silence – made more urgent by the resonance of the alloy block and cylinder head. Overhead valves were pushrod driven, and for the first and only time an Armstrong Siddeley six-cylinder engine ran on seven main bearings. A vibration damper attached to the nose of the crankshaft was concealed within the timing case. Although contemporary sales material seldom quoted power output or torque figures, as reported in *The Motor* of March 21, 1933 the engine developed around 125bhp at 3200rpm, and on a final drive ratio of about 3.6:1 was geared for 60mph at 2500rpm in top.

Following usual company practice, there was a short shaft from the flywheel to the separately mounted preselector gearbox, which drove the rear axle via a stout tailshaft within a torque tube. Gearchanging was from the outset servo assisted, and the Mark II cars were additionally fitted with a clutch to render take-off and gearchanges even silkier than previously. Despite a very tall initial final drive ratio, the lightest of the cars were able to run from a walking pace to more than 90mph on top gear, reportedly without quiver or noise. Final drive ratios ranged from a low of 4.1:1 to a high of 3.64:1, and attainable maximum speeds varied accordingly.

The chassis was largely conventional but extremely strong, and in early form was available in two wheelbase lengths – 11' and 12'; a longer wheelbase of 11'3½" was used for the Mark II short-wheelbase cars.

Four wheel Bendix semi-servo brakes were initially offered, all shoes in all four wheels operated by footbrake and handbrake, as on the later 18/20hp cars; the Mark II cars (built after May, 1935) used a Dewandre vacuum servo to further lighten braking loads, rendering these large cars more manageable. Even the shorter wheelbase closed cars weighed more than two tons, so all help was welcomed.

The Special was in any form an imposing vehicle, bodied chiefly by in-house coachbuilder Burlington, but displaying some spectacular works by outsiders including Barker, Cross & Ellis, Gurney Nutting, Hooper, Lancefield, Mulliner, Park Ward (their Touring Saloon on the shorter wheelbase strongly resembling an up-scaled Derby Bentley), Salmons Tickford, Thrupp & Maberley and Vanden Plas. In the bespoke manner, all were available with equipment to the customer's requirements – including colours – although 'standard' specifications existed for each model.

The last of 253 examples was built in January, 1937, although new cars were sold by dealers into 1938. It is easy to dismiss the Special as its maker's folly, but Siddeley's desire to build a top-quality model is entirely consistent with his previous attempts to cover all market sectors – a policy implemented from day one. He was not alone in seeking to market lavish and costly luxury cars in the midst of the

Depression, since the Special was sold alongside patricians like the Phantom III Rolls-Royce and K6 Hispano Suiza, the V16 Marmon and Cadillac, the SJ Duesenberg, the Packard 8 and 12, the D8 Delage and the 12-cylinder Delahaye – and was frequently comparable in build quality and performance.

While many of the mentioned marques went to the wall after the commercial failure of such cars, Armstrong Siddeley survived thanks to the market coverage of its smaller models, and it is ironic that the humble 12hp probably saved the company from financial oblivion when the Special was bleeding money.

The motoring press raved about the Special from its introduction, *The Motor* in its edition of March 21, 1933, saying: "One of the most impressive features about the car is the extreme ease with which it is handled. We know of many so-called 'baby' vehicles that are no lighter to steer or to manoeuvre than this fine, big, full-sized motorcar. At any speed from a crawl to over 80mph on top gear, the steering is easy and accurate. The gear-changing pedal is light to operate, the Bendix brakes come on smoothly and powerfully at the slightest touch,

Preliminary brochure cover image for the 1933 model range catalogue, depicting the yet-to-be-released Siddeley Special.

133

while even the spring on the accelerator pedal is no heavier than is absolutely necessary.

"The car is steady at all speeds, even on rough road surfaces. Indeed, when meeting another vehicle at speed on a fairly narrow road, one can safely steer almost into the gutter, ignoring bumps and pot-holes, without the steering being affected in the slightest. Consequently, 60 m.p.h. is an easy, effortless, cruising speed. One just sits back comfortably, holding the wheel loosely, completely at ease".

Publicity material was happy to quote owners' opinions, amongst them the following from Sir Malcolm Campbell, writing in January, 1935: "The Siddeley Special which I have owned for over eighteen months and which has been in constant use, has afforded me every possible satisfaction.

"The car is capable of very fine performance on the road, and its stability on corners and greasy roads is really remarkable. The suspension is another noteworthy feature, affording as it does the maximum amount of comfort to the passengers using the back

seat." Sir Malcolm's praise is the more noteworthy since the Siddeley followed his purchase of one of the first Bentley 3½ litre cars, which he quickly sold.

W F Bradley, continental correspondent for *The Autocar*, in July, 1933 drove an open Special to survey for the Automobile Association their proposed trunk road from London to Istanbul in Turkey. Together with his daughter and one Bill Whitlock from the works' Finished Test Department, they completed the 4000-mile journey without incident or failure.

Another paeon of praise concluded: "The car is luxuriously comfortable at all speeds, I do indeed congratulate you on a really fine car. It is undoubtedly the finest car on the road without any exception and I write as one who has experience of most makes of the better cars over a twenty year period". And one last word: "The performance and appearance are exceptional, one of its most remarkable features is the effortless way in which it covers long distances".

Below: Brochure image of the early Special Burlington Sports Saloon, handsome in light grey, and offered for £865.

Below right: Offside view of the Special's five-litre engine.

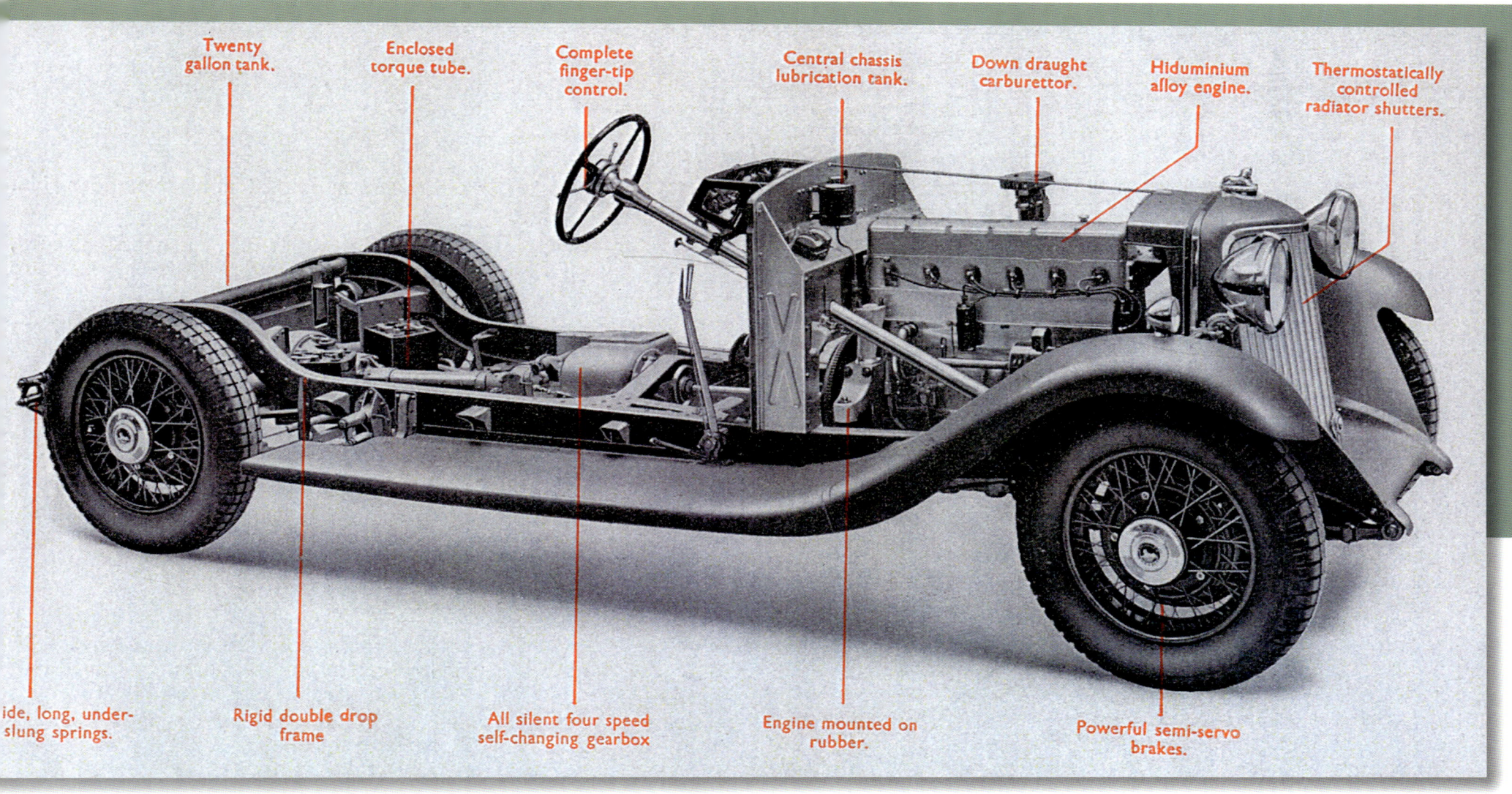

Twenty gallon tank.

Enclosed torque tube.

Complete finger-tip control.

Central chassis lubrication tank.

Down draught carburettor.

Hiduminium alloy engine.

Thermostatically controlled radiator shutters.

ide, long, under-slung springs.

Rigid double drop frame

All silent four speed self-changing gearbox

Engine mounted on rubber.

Powerful semi-servo brakes.

Brochure image of the Special chassis, noting its features.

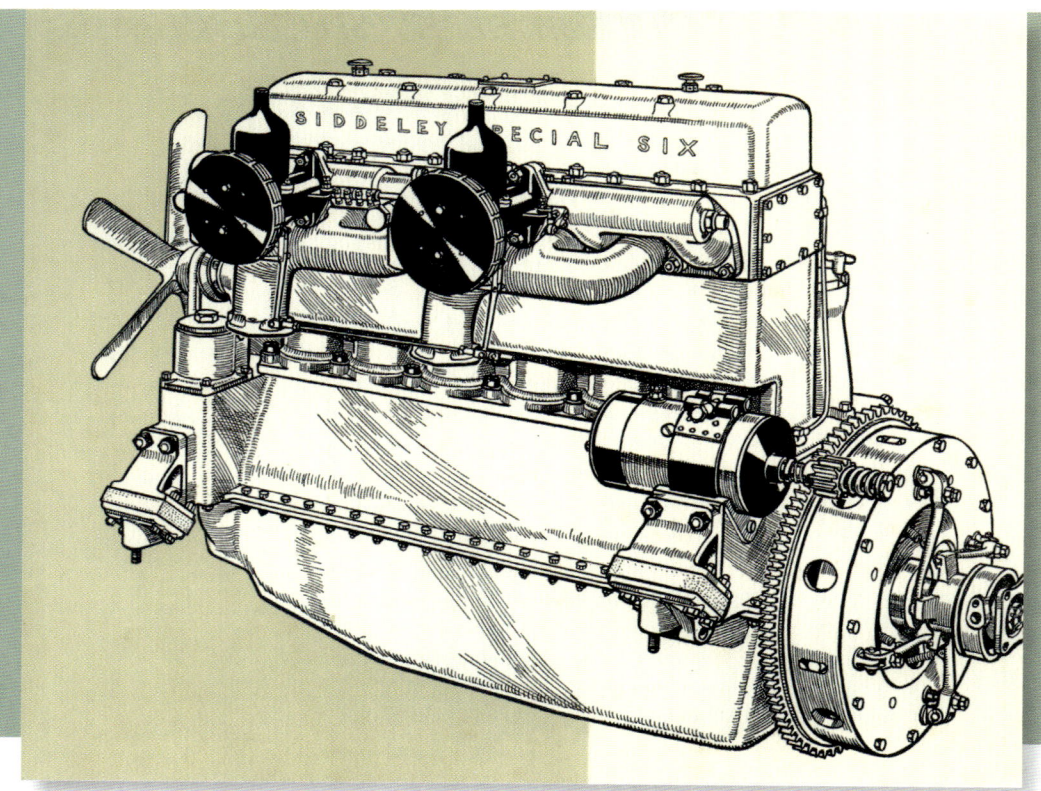

Above: Nearside view of the engine showing the dual SU carburettors fitted shortly after production began.

Right: Schematic drawing showing the vacuum assistance mechanism for the gearchange pedal, unique to the Special.

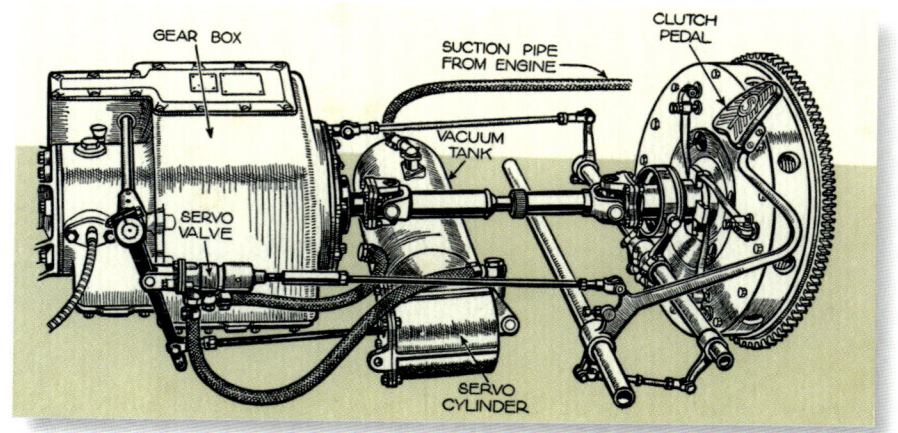

Exotic car, exotic location. *The Autocar* correspondent, W. F. Bradley, drove this splendid open Special from London to Istanbul in 1933, surveying a proposed new road for the Automobile Association.

Very early production Special Vanden Plas tourer on the short chassis, driven by H. E. Symons in the 1933 RAC Rally.
The following car, wearing the Siddeley family number plate A52, is a Salmons Foursome coupé driven by Cyril Siddeley, son of JDS.

Above: The Special's designer, Fred Allard, reunited with his creation in 1957.

Right: Works photograph of the Burlington Sports Saloon. Note the wheel discs covering the wire wheels of this early car.

Top: Early series Burlington Special Sports Saloon, showing the truncated luggage compartment, lengthened and softened on the Mark II version of this body.

Above: Open coachwork was rare on the Special in any form. Here is a brochure illustration of the Vanden Plas Open Tourer, priced at £900 including special equipment such as permanent jacks and bumpers.

With best wishes
from
Malcolm Campbell
23/10/33.

Above: The open cars were the lightest and fastest of the Specials. This Vanden Plas tourer was tested by *The Motor* at 94mph.

Left: Land Speed Record ace Sir Malcolm Campbell used – but may not have owned – this early Burlington Special Sports Saloon in 1933.

This open Special Vanden Plas tourer was a factory demonstrator, posed with a less powerful stablemate and Siddeley family members.

Top: Brochure illustration of an early Special with Coupé/Cabriolet coachwork by Salmons & Sons. This imposing car was offered for £945 in 1934.

Above: Brochure illustrations showed some adventurous colour schemes available on the Specials. In fact colour was to customer choice.

Left: Brochure illustration depicting the Mark II Sports Saloon by Bur ington.

Top: Handsome D-back limousine on the long Special chassis, probably built by Burlington.

Right: Brochure illustration of the Burlington limousine.

This superb Limousine DeVille
Special was constructed to the
order of Warwick Wright Ltd
by The Lancefield Coachworks,
and offered at £1360.

Main: Brochure illustration of a Special with Limousine DeVille coachwork, builder not identified.

Left: Burlington's Special Touring Limousine.

Far left and left: Lancefield also designed and built this Streamlined Saloon on the short Special chassis. It was presented at the 1934 RAC Rally coachwork competition.

Left: Swashbuckling Special all-weather tourer, built by an unknown coachbuilder.

Left: Elegant and purposeful, this Special wears an Australian two-door coupé body built by the Sydney firm of E. W. Creswell. Sydney, New South Wales dealer Buckle Motors delivered this car to Mr S. E. Chatterton on 20th February, 1934.

Above: Magnificent Teutonic Special with sports coupé coachwork by Vanden Plas.

Left: Fortunate Sydney, Australia doctor, C. Eder George, with his Mark II Special on the 11'4" chassis, with fully-imported Sports Saloon coachwork by Burlington. This car was one of several Armstrong Siddeleys owned by the doctor and his family, and was delivered new by Buckle Motors.

October 16, 1935.

The Motor 53

Mark II Series. *Sports Saloon* £1,050

The Siddeley Special Sports Saloon challenges comparison

RESTRAINED, dignified carriagework on a car designed on aero engine principles to give the finest performance that the experience of aircraft engineers can produce, the Mark II Siddeley Special Sports Saloon is a most attractive model. For long distance driving its performance is exceptional yet for town work it has a luxury and distinction which is all its own. May we arrange for you an extended trial run?

Other Models
Touring Limousine
£1,300
Enclosed Limousine
or Landaulette
£1,360

PLEASE WRITE FOR
CATALOGUE
"SH.163"

SIDDELEY
SPECIAL
Mark II Series
With Coachwork by Burlington

ARMSTRONG SIDDELEY MOTORS LIMITED, COVENTRY

MANCHESTER: 35 KING STREET WEST

LONDON: 10 OLD BOND STREET, W.1

Agents in all principal centres

BUY A CAR MADE IN THE UNITED KINGDOM

KINDLY MENTION "THE MOTOR" WHEN CORRESPONDING WITH ADVERTISERS.

63

Advertisement for the Special Mark II from October, 1935. Note that prices had risen significantly from the time of the Special's introduction.

Factory designation	Siddeley Special	Siddeley Special Mark II
Date introduced	March 1933	May 1935
Motor type	6-cyl 4-stroke in-line water-cooled ohv	same
Dimensions	88.9 X 133.4mm = 4960cc	same
Power/rpm	125bhp @ 3200rpm	same
Fuel feed	mech pump from tank to Claudel Hobson downdraught	
	carb, changed to dual SU sidedraught carbs (1934)	same
Ignition	battery & coil	same
Transmission type	4-spd & Rev Wilson preselector, vacuum assisted	same
Ratios	13.37 7.7 5.0 3.6:1 (short) 13.8 8.51 5.47 3.75 (Long)	
Final drive ratio	3.6:1 (short) 3.75:1 (Long)	same
Clutch		Newton centrifugal
Steering		
Suspension		
Front	semi-elliptic springs, cabin-adjustable Luvax dampers	same
Rear	cantilever springs, cabin-adjustable Luvax dampers	same
Brakes	14" semi-servo drums all round	same plus Dewandre vacuum servo
Wheels	steel discs or bolt-on wires	same
Tyres	6.50 X 20" cross ply	6.50 X 19" cross ply
Dimensions		
Wheelbase	11' (long 12')	11'3½" (long same 12')
Track front	4'8"	
Track rear	4'8"	
Overall length	15'7" (chassis) 16'5¾" (tourer)	dependent on body style & coachbuilder
Overall width	5'9"	same
Height	dependent on body style & coachbuilder	same
Unladen weight	tourer 38 cwt, sports saloon 46 cwt	same, weights varying according to body style & coachwork
Factory coachwork	enclosed limousine or landaulette, sports saloon	sports saloon, touring limousine, 7-str limousine or landaulette
Variants	per outside coachbuilders, incl Barker, Charlesworth, Cross & Ellis, Gurney Nutting, Lancefield, Martin Walter, Mayfair, A & H J Mulliner, Vanden Plas	
Performance		
Max speed (mph)	93 (tourer) 85 (sports saloon) 80+ (limousine)	similar
Fuel consumption (mpg)	12-15 depending on coachwork	similar
Number produced	253 (total both series) – 76 built by coachbuilders other than Burlington	
Prices	(1933) limousine/landaulette £1250	(1935) sports saloon £965-£1050, touring limousine £1300, limousine £1360
Date last produced	October 1934	January 1937

CHAPTER vii

THE SEVENTEEN HP
1934-1938

Although evolved from the side-valve Fifteen that it replaced, the Seventeen during its relatively short production life encompassed so many significant developments that it warrants its own model chapter.

Heart of the new model was its overhead valve six-cylinder engine, with bores of 66.67mm and sharing the 114mm stroke of the last Fifteen. The forged one-piece crankshaft ran in four white-metal bearings and was counterbalanced. There was a downdraught Claudel Hobson carburettor (supplanted by a Zenith unit in 1937) and a front-mounted belt-driven cooling fan, while the dynamo was still turned by the timing chain. Displacing 2394cc this engine developed 63bhp at 3500rpm in all its forms. The shortest wheelbase cars, being also the lightest, would reach more than 70mph and return around 22mpg at touring speeds.

All models used worm-and-nut steering gear, four wheel brakes operated by cables, semi-elliptic springs all round with Luvax hydraulic shock absorbers, centralised chassis lubrication, permanently fixed DWS jacks, and the option of bolt-on wire wheels or steel discs. Initially the Short chassis cars were offered with 5.25 X 19" wires as standard, but the Standard wheelbase used 5.25 X 17" wires or discs, with larger 6.00 X 17" covers on the Long cars. These specifications changed as the model evolved.

The transmission – always a four-speed preselector unit – was initially located as previously on its own cross-member and attached to the flywheel by a short shaft. From early 1936 the cars were fitted with the Newton centrifugal clutch, which allowed the engine to idle in gear while stationary, gave smooth take-up from rest as it engaged, and permitted the first gear drum and band to be reduced in size – since no longer need they take the torque of starts in first gear 'on the bands'.

With much fanfare the company then styled its connection of engine to transmission as 'Balanced Drive' in 1937, and issued wordy explanations of this development in booklets which stretched the spin-doctor's art. British cars, chiefly high quality models, retained separately-mounted gearboxes far longer than even bread-and-butter models from the Continent and the States, perhaps for ease of major service to engine or gearbox, but maybe clinging to some obscure image of exclusivity (in the same way that, in the 1920s, the length of an unsupported steering column was meant to denote the quality of the car, a myth undone by the fact that the Fiat 501's column was longer than that on a Rolls-Royce Silver Ghost).

However long it may have taken Armstrong Siddeley to discover the convenience of the bell-housing, designers took the opportunity to render the whole power transmission unit lighter, smoother and more efficient. The company had long used heavy vaned flywheels to subdue vibrations, from their Thirty until midway through the lifespan of the Fifteen, before engines were routinely balanced upon assembly.

Connection of a transmission comprising a series of rotating metal drums meant that flywheel size and weight could be reduced, rendering the engines more lively. Fitment of the traffic clutch made the cars much easier to manage, and gave to the driver enhanced ability to make best use of available power. But the Seventeen Touring Saloon took 35 seconds to reach 60mph on test, which was hardly high performance. The short-wheelbase Foursome was markedly quicker, taking 28¾ seconds for the same test.

Three chassis lengths were eventually employed – the Short 17 on a 9'3" wheelbase, the Standard 17 on 9'8", and the Long 17 (introduced late in 1935) on 10'3 ½"; the Short used a track width of 4'4", the others 4'8" until 1938, when they were increased by one inch. Development of each type followed divergent paths due to particular problems experienced with a combination of the new ohv engine, and changes to the engine and radiator's forward location. The engine no longer served as a stressed member of the frame, and was mounted on rubber at four points.

The shortest wheelbase frame was least developed and probably the most satisfactory, its strength helped by the addition of stout torque rods running from the front axle to the front dumb-irons, which stiffened the front assembly under heavy braking and cornering. From October, 1937, in Mark II form it used a modified chassis in which the structural strength of the side- and cross-members was helped by the inclusion of box sections – a practice also applied to the longer frames.

The Standard and Long frames required early attention to reduce front-end shake and the transmission of engine vibrations, despite the

introduction of heavy pressed box sections forward and a separate cross member aft of the engine. The Standard chassis was introduced on a lengthened version of the Short 17 in October, 1934, but was replaced by a modified version in December of that year. In the interests of greater passenger comfort in those cars destined to be bodied as large saloons or limousines, the rear passengers were moved forward of the rear axle line, and the engine and radiator moved forward to accommodate the change while retaining legroom in the front compartment. The separate mounting of the engine called for strengthening plates to control shimmy, and harmonic bumpers were also tried front and rear. The move in January, 1936, to a box-reinforced frame finally cured the vibration problem.

As previously, the factory offered a wide range of coachwork styles, continuing the line of handsome two door four seaters called the Foursomes, the D-back saloons and limousines, and the very attractively modern Atalanta. This handsome four-light saloon was reportedly designed by Cyril Siddeley, and was named after the Atalanta passenger aircraft built by Armstrong Whitworth for Imperial Airways, used on their Cairo-Cape Town service. Only a handful of open tourers were built and briefly catalogued, while outside coachbuilders were supplied with chassis on which some notably attractive bodies were built. The new Touring Saloon added a short luggage compartment to the established coachbuilt saloon, producing a somewhat awkward rear treatment similar to that on contemporary Austin and Wolseley models.

Above left and above: Nearside and offside cf the 17hp engine. Note the belt-driven fan, coil ignition and oil filter. The dynamo and water pump were still driven from the timing case.

Sales material proudly boasted that the new compartment could carry two sets of golf clubs.

Production methods favoured lightness toward the end of the model's life, with changes to materials used for items like seat frames and trim boards contributing to savings of up to 150lbs in overall weight, reflected in improved performance.

Contemporary assessments of the model were consistently favourable, especially when describing the semi-sporting versions built on the shortest chassis. *The Autocar* of May 3rd, 1935, said: "It is (a car) in which a state of affairs has been achieved whereby a modern kind of performance is matched by ease of handling, and a balance has been arrived at throughout the car.

"To take one aspect alone, it has the happy facility of being entirely suited to a driver whose principal need may be for running in and around town, since it is flexible on top gear, quiet mechanically and distinguished in appearance; yet it is full well able to satisfy the same driver when he is in a hurry to cover long distances quickly and easily, for the natural speed is quite fast and the ultimate maximum usefully high".

Describing the Seventeen Touring Saloon in their issue of February 8th, 1936, *The Practical Motorist* caught the essence of Armstrong Siddeley cars of the 'thirties when they said: "Armstrong Siddeley coachwork has always been acknowledged to be of extremely high quality, and every body bears the mark of having been individually built. In fact, it is probably their exclusive carriage-work which gives Armstrong Siddeley cars their peculiar distinction and dignity".

The Seventeen was an altogether more modern and sprightly car than the Fifteen it replaced, its shorter-wheelbase models paving the way for the abandonment of the chauffeur and the universal production of owner-driven models which were livelier and easier to drive than their predecessors.

Lavish interior fittings of the limousine, on the relatively modest long 17hp chassis.

Above: The Burlington Coachbuilt Saloon on the standard wheelbase.

Above: The Burlington 7-seater limousine/landaulette on the longest of the three wheelbases offered.

Above: The particularly handsome Foursome two-door four-seat saloon on the shortest chassis.

Above: Also on the Short 17 chassis was the four-light four-door saloon.

The modern and handsome Atalanta body style by Burlington was
offered on both the 17hp and 20hp chassis.

Above: This body style was also available on several chassis, Burlington's Town and Country saloon providing a wind-down glass division between the front and rear compartments.

Above: The late series limousine retained the D-back of the earlier car, and was available only on the longest wheelbase.

Top: As before, interior fittings bordered on the lavish, with folding occasional seats trimmed in fine leather, foot-rails, rugs and deeply upholstered rear seats. For a modestly-sized motor car, the 17hp limousine provided a degree of opulence not found in competitors of similar size.

Left: The Burlington six-light saloon was built on the standard chassis, yet still retained the presence and dignity of the longer cars.

Above left and right: Interior of the six-light saloon continued the make's reputation for 'Motor Carriages of Perfect Comfort', with foot-rails, over-rugs and folding polished timber picnic tables.

Armstrong Siddeley under four Kings

A Tradition for fine cars

"The" Motor

Prices from £320 · £1360.

May 4, 1937.

160

Above: The last body style offered on the 17hp standard chassis was the Touring Saloon, which repeated the awkward tail treatment designed to provide enclosed luggage accommodation.

Opposite page: Company advertisement for the 17hp in the 'Coronation & Whitsun Number' of *The Motor*, May 4, 1937.

Above: However awkward Burlington's Touring Saloon may have appeared, it was no match for this 17hp with saloon coachwork by Ruskin of Melbourne. The company specialised in building clones of bodies attached to American-made cars like Chevrolet, Buick and Dodge, from which this unfortunate style was evidently derived.

Factory designation	17hp
Date introduced	Olympia Motor Show, October 1934
Motor type	6-cyl 4-stroke in-line water-cooled ohv
Dimensions	66.67 X 114mm = 2394cc
Fuel feed	AC mech pump from rear tank to Claudel Hobson carb. Zenith downdraught carb from October 1937
Ignition	battery & coil with automatic advance/retard control
Transmission type	4-spd & Rev Wilson gearbox. From October 1937 'box in unit with the engine
Ratios	(short) 20.4 11.65 7.5 5.1 (standard) 21.2 12.1 7.8 5.3 (long) 22 12.57 8.1 5.5:1
Final drive ratio	(short) 5.1:1 (standard) 5.3:1 (long) 5.5:1
Clutch	Newton centrifugal clutch from October 1936
Steering	worm & nut
Suspension	
Front	gaitered semi-elliptic springs, Luvax hydraulic dampers
Rear	underslung gaitered semi-elliptic springs, Luvax hydraulic dampers
Brakes	4-whl semi-servo drum brakes, cable operated
Wheels	steel disc or bolt on wires 19" on short wheelbase, 17" on longer wheelbases
Tyres	(short) 5.25 X 19" (standard) 5.50 X 17" (long) 6.00 X 17"
Dimensions	
Wheelbase	(short) 9'3" (standard) 9'8" (long) 10' 3½"
Track front	(short) 4'4" (standard & long) 4'9"
Track rear	(short) 4'4" (standard & long) 4'9"
Overall length	(short) 14'2" (standard) 15'3" (long) 15'6"
Overall width	(short) 5'4" (standard & long) 5'9"
Height	dependent on body style & coachbuilder
Unladen weight	sports foursome 28 cwt
Factory coachwork	sports foursome, 6-lt coachbuilt & 4-lt sports saloons, tourer, limousine/landaulette
Variants	per outside coachbuilders
Performance	
Max speed (mph)	sports foursome 72 (Autocar test #940) 6-lt saloon 68.7
Fuel consumption (mpg)	21-22
Number produced	(short 17) 1250 (standard 17) 3453 (long 17) 408
Prices	(1935) sports foursome £385 coachbuilt saloon & open tourer £465 sports saloon£495
	(1936) foursome £385 4-lt saloon £425 6-lt touring saloon £475 4-lt Atalanta saloon £525 7-seat limousine or landaulette £585
Date last produced	(short) November 1938 (standard) March 1939 (long) April 1939

THE SAGA OF THE PRESELECTOR GEARBOX, FLUID FLYWHEEL AND CENTRIFUGAL CLUTCH

The preselector gearbox as designed and patented by Walter Wilson had its roots in the partnership of Wilson and Percy Sinclair Pilcher, who launched the firm of Wilson-Pilcher Ltd in 1897. Pilcher was an eccentric pioneer aviator who built a series of man-powered gliders, and enthused about the possibilities of steam-driven aircraft. Wilson designed advanced and flexibly mounted horizontally-opposed engines connected to epicyclic transmissions, and produced cars under the Wilson-Pilcher name from 1901, although Pilcher had by then fallen victim to one of his own gliders. By 1904 the company was destitute, and was purchased by Armstrong Whitworth.

Wilson continued work on his epicyclic gearbox, and in 1921 convinced Vauxhall Motors to install its prototype in a new 14-40 car, under the supervision of Laurence Pomeroy. On test the transmission was deemed a success, and Pomeroy was enthusiastic about its manufacture and installation in his cars. But financial strictures and the acquisition of Vauxhall by General Motors in 1925 ended any further collaboration.

In 1927 John Siddeley and Walter Wilson discussed their joint development and manufacture of the Wilson epicyclic gearbox, and incorporated Improved Gears Ltd in December, 1928. Wilson assigned his patents to the new company, while Siddeley injected capital to the value of £5000.

The preselector gearbox was offered on the Armstrong Siddeley 20hp car in 1928, and the option was quickly extended to other models in the range. Whilst it was a huge improvement on the conventional crash gearbox, drivers either depressed the change pedal or engaged neutral when stopping. Siddeley wanted some device to automatically disengage drive when the car was stationary.

That device was the fluid coupling. In 1905, Dr Hermann Föttinger patented his fluid coupling and a torque converter. These would not function with conventional

transmissions, but Harold Sinclair patented his redesign in February, 1928, after experimenting with fluid couplings installed in London buses; Daimler began building the couplings and fitting them to their cars and buses.

Armstrong Siddeley supplied Wilson transmissions, and Improved Gears later licensed Daimler to build and install them in their vehicles. From 1930 the Daimler-sourced fluid flywheel was offered for £50 extra on the 30hp and Special 20hp cars, and Siddeley had one fitted to his personal 30hp. The fluid flywheel significantly sweetened take-up and gearchanges, even though its principle meant some power loss.

Daimler and Managing Director Percy Martin had meanwhile successfully applied for a patent covering the combination of the Wilson gearbox with the fluid flywheel, without prior notice to Siddeley or Wilson. Although Siddeley had been outmanoeuvred by Martin, Wilson pursued commercial gain for Improved Gears Ltd, and clashed with Siddeley when Humber requested a licence to manufacture preselector gearboxes for their cars, which Siddeley vetoed. He and Wilson did not speak for four years, and Humber never received their licence.

Daimler ceased supply of fluid flywheels in 1933, and Siddeley looked elsewhere for an intermediate mechanism to perform a similar function. He still wanted to employ some form of interface between his cars' engines and their preselective transmissions, allowing the vehicles to be brought to rest in traffic merely by applying the foot-brake. He secured supply of the simpler centrifugal automatic clutch designed by Noel Newton, which had the added advantage of transmitting power without loss.

Newton was the son of Manchester motor trader John Newton, who re-badged Italian-made SCAT cars in 1913-1914 as Newton-Bennett, and later manufactured automotive components under the name of Newton & Bennett. The "traffic clutch" was fitted to all Armstrong Siddeley cars with preselector gearboxes from 1937 to 1958.

The tale reveals the incestuous nature of very early motor manufacturing in Britain, and probably goes some way to explaining Siddeley's refusal to assist Rolls-Royce to resolve difficulties with the hydraulic valve tappets on their Phantom III, when those on the Siddeley Special functioned satisfactorily.

Above: The Newton centrifugal clutch attached to a 17hp engine.

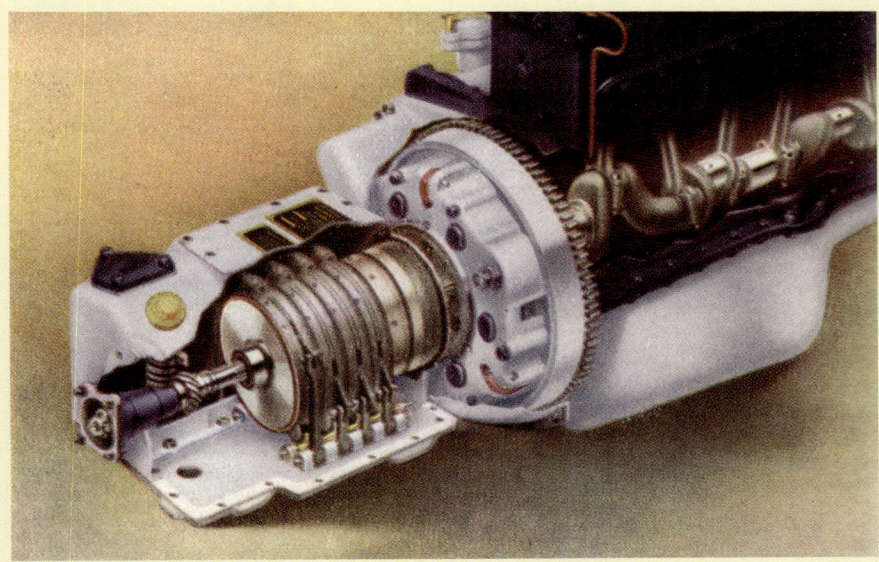

Above: After 1937, the preselector gearbox was attached to the engine and the centrifugal clutch, in what was termed 'Balanced Drive'.

THE PRE-WAR SIXTEEN
1938-1941

"**N**o Armstrong Siddeley previously has performed in relation to its engine size as this new 16hp model does. It is expressing the position mildly to state that a surprise is received within a few miles of getting into the car as a stranger". The new model was thereby welcomed by *The Autocar* in its issue of September 23, 1938.

Hon Maynard Greville wrote in *Country Life* on December 31, 1938 that: "The 16hp Armstrong Siddeley should prove most popular, as though it is a roomy family car it has a brisk performance and its size makes for economical running. Its general performance and behaviour came as a pleasant surprise as it retains all the old features which have made the Armstrong Siddeley famous throughout the world, and added to these certain very modern and desirable attributes".

And John Oliver wrote in *The Tatler* of December 7, 1938: "The traffic clutch enables the driver to creep or to catapult forward according to his wish or whim...The suspension is good, when cruising at 65mph, the car is comfortable and easy-moving...At the end of a three-hundred-mile run, driver and passengers will like it as well as, or better than, when they started". While reports and tests of new model Armstrong Siddeley cars were always positive in their home country, such comments on the new Sixteen conveyed consistent enthusiasm.

This was the newest new Armstrong Siddeley since 1919, excepting only the stand-out Siddeley Special. Its 65X100mm six cylinder overhead valve engine was entirely new, for the first time employing a relatively short stroke which reduced piston speeds but retained a good mix of torque and top-end power. Tuning specialist Harry Weslake advised on cylinder head design (he was still consulting on such matters as late as the second series Rover Three Litre of 1962), with particular reference to carburation and porting. The carburettor was a downdraught Zenith, but otherwise engine ancillaries followed the lead of the Seventeen which it replaced. The crankshaft was carefully balanced as a unit with flywheel and transmission. Belt drive was employed for dynamo, water pump and fan, and the engine was mounted to the frame by rubber at four points.

The chassis was a very modern unit, appearing almost as a unitary platform, so all-enclosing were the strengthening plates joining the side rails, with a tunnel for the now-open tailshaft. Suspension retained semi-elliptic springs underslung at the rear and reverse-cambered at the front, assisted by Luvax double piston shock absorbers. Brakes were

Girling self-compensating units operated by cable, there was centralised chassis lubrication, and the Jackall hydraulic jacking system superseded the DWS mechanical units. Steering was by Burman Douglas worm-and-nut gear, while wheels were styled steel discs running on 5.50 X 17" tyres. Everywhere was the whiff of 'new broom'.

Equipment levels equalled usual company practice, and included on all models foglamps, front and rear bumpers, sliding steel sunroof, wind deflectors and self-cancelling trafficators as standard.

The new car reached 73.77mph on test, with speeds of 20, 36 and 57mph on the indirects. From rest to 50mph took 17.4 seconds – then a highly respectable performance for a 5/6 seater weighing 27cwt dry.

While the huge majority were bodied by the factory, the attractive four-light saloon resembling the gracious Atalanta style was initially built by Arthur Mulliner, and small numbers of chassis were supplied to Charlesworth and Salmons Tickford.

Despite the onset of World War 2 in September, 1939, production of the Sixteen continued at the Manchester and London works of Henlys, one of the company's main dealers, to whom supplies of all spares were entrusted. Henlys continued to build handfuls of 16hp and 25hp cars until late 1943 under the auspices of the Ministry of War Transport, many of the cars serving as staff cars and conveyances for senior military and Government personnel. That 961 examples of the Sixteen found buyers during its truncated model run speaks of its qualities and ready market acceptance. Its engine survived the war to power the post-war Sixteen.

Indicative of the car's reception by the buying public, just a couple of the testimonials published in company sales literature of late 1939 were: "I have driven Armstrong Siddeley cars for 25 years and the new 16hp car for over 3000 miles. In my opinion the performance of the car far exceeds any other model of your make that I have handled. I think this car is more into line with other makers of similar power. The pick-up is distinctly good and the braking good".

And, tellingly at a time when the owner-driven quality car was in its ascendancy: "My Chauffeur says that during the last twelve years he has driven Armstrong Siddeley cars of 30hp, 20hp and 15hp, and now their new 16hp, and in his opinion this new car has the performance and power of the 30hp. For my own part, I may say that in comfort it compares favourably with all the others".

An early casualty of the war was the uprated 20hp model which followed a similar pattern to the new Sixteen. Included in sales brochures from September, 1938, the all-new Twenty was the first Armstrong Siddeley to include independent front suspension, on the André Girling system, with coils, wishbones and dampers. The engine had bores of 77mm and stroke of 105mm – even closer to square than the Sixteen – displacing a useful 2780cc. In September *The Autocar* described three different versions of the new Twenty which, together with its inclusion in the company catalogue, showed its development was nearing completion. A complete chassis was displayed unclothed at the October, 1938 Olympia Motor Show.

While reasons for its abandonment are disputed, in early 1939 Nazi Germany annexed Czechoslovakia, and the Chairman of Hawker Siddeley, Sir T O M Sopwith, felt sufficiently uneasy about gathering war clouds that he committed the company to major production capacity for Hurricane fighter aircraft. This move drained available development finance for car production and presaged new priorities at Parkside. The undoubted success of the smaller Sixteen may in itself have impacted on the Board's decision on 22nd March, 1939, to abandon the Twenty, and to ultimately scrap or dismantle the handful of cars already assembled.

An independently sprung Armstrong Siddeley would have to await the new Sixteen introduced immediately after the war.

Above: New look for a thoroughly modern car. The Sixteen broke with many of the company's traditions, while retaining its emphasis on quality and comfort.

Right: The very attractive 16hp Touring Saloon was as handsome as contemporary quality cars such as Alvis. As previously the coachwork was by Burlington.

- Exceptional power attained by cylinder head design, following aero engine experience, to give the most efficient distribution of vapourised mixture ensuring easy starting and clean, smooth pick-up throughout the range.
- Dynamically counter-balanced four-bearing crankshaft.
- Detachable strip-metal bearings fitted to connecting rods and main bearings.
- Pressure-fed lubrication to all bearings, camshaft and valve rockers

New 16 h.p. Chassis

- Sealed floor fume-proof chassis.
- Body bolted to frame making special box section to give rigidity and lightness.
- Rigid front-end carrying engine mounted on rubber.
- Balanced Drive incorporating engine, automatic clutch and self-changing gears.
- Reverse cambered suspension giving easy ride with maximum stability.
- Self-compensating easily adjustable brakes.
- Automatic lubrication throughout.
- Quick filling 11-gallon petrol tank with reserve tap.

The 16hp chassis broke much new ground, especially with its fabricated strengthening platform and open tailshaft.

169

Right: Newly informal interior
of the light and airy Touring
Saloon.

Left: Like the chassis, the 16hp
engine was clean, modern.
Belt drive was used for fan,
water pump and dynamo.

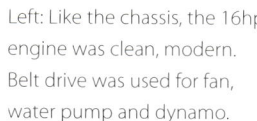

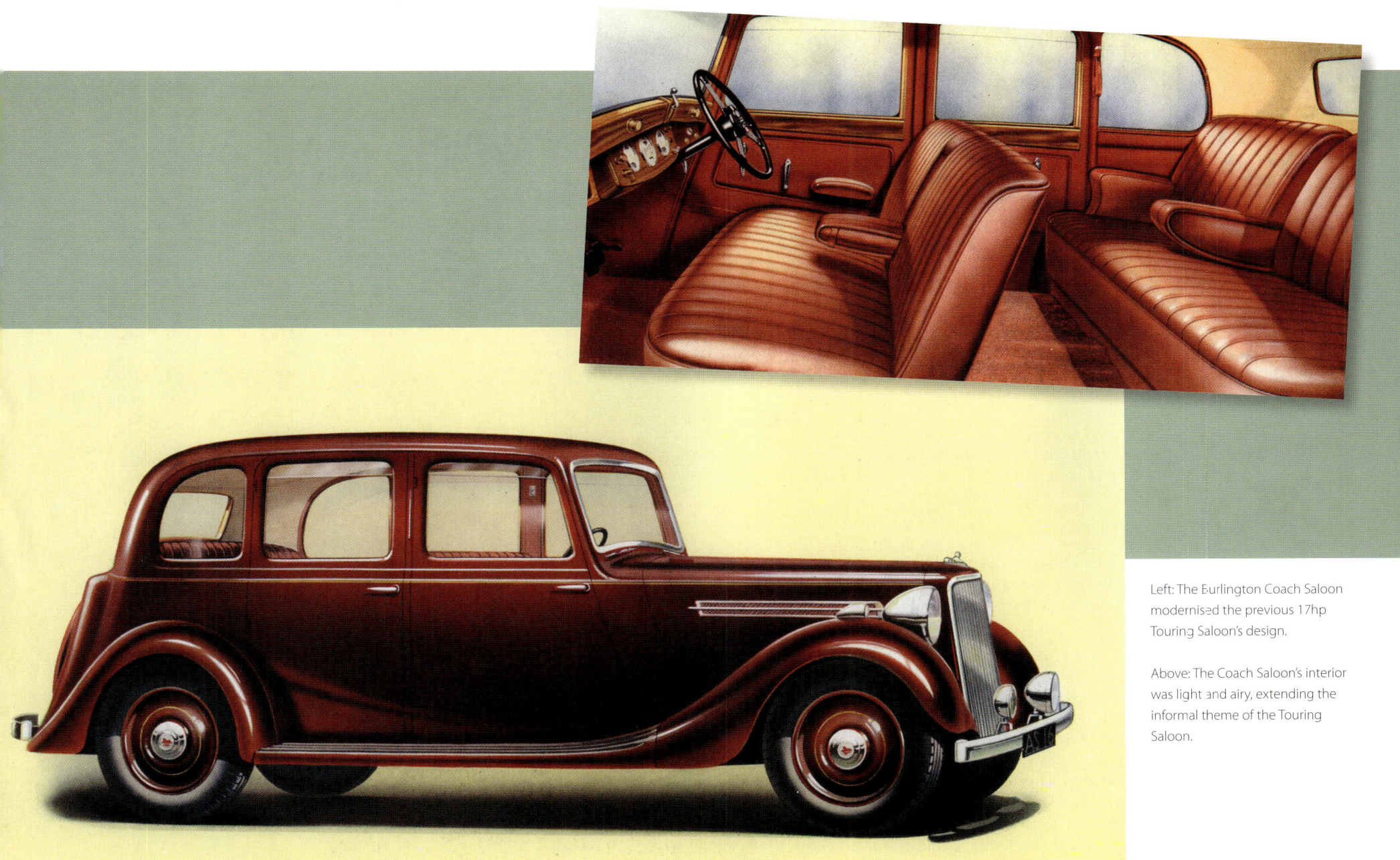

Left: The Burlington Coach Saloon modernised the previous 17hp Touring Saloon's design.

Above: The Coach Saloon's interior was light and airy, extending the informal theme of the Touring Saloon.

Above: Modern facia and plenty of window area of the 16hp meant safety as well as passenger convenience.

Right: On the Coach Saloon the spare wheel was carried inside the boot-lid, thereby avoiding wasted luggage space.

Far right: This advertisement from April, 1939 stressed value-for-money. The 16hp was certainly well equipped, and at £380 for the Touring or Coach Saloon competed strongly against its other British quality rivals.

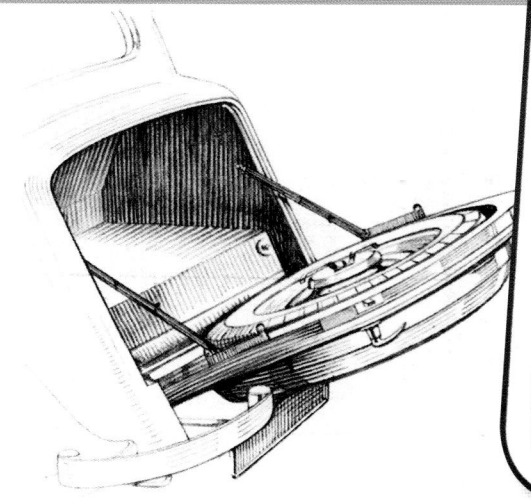

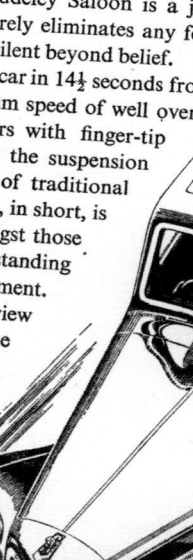

172

- Cylinder head entirely redesigned following aero engine practice to give increased efficiency and power output.
- Four-bearing dynamically counterbalanced crankshaft sets new standard of smoothness.
- Detachable strip-metal bearings.
- Pressure lubrication by crankshaft driven pump.

New 20 h.p. Chassis

- Body bolted to frame making special box section to give rigidity and lightness.
- Andre-Girling independent front wheel suspension.
- Balanced Drive incorporating self-changing gear, automatic clutch and engine in one unit.
- Self-compensating brakes.
- Automatic lubrication using engine oil.
- Special dashboard design providing for extraction of under-bonnet heat and fumes.

Sad postscript. The model range catalogue for September, 1938 contained technical details, specifications, illustrations and even prices for an enlarged version of the 16hp – the 20hp – whose principal feature was the company's first venture into independent front suspension. This chassis illustration shows that the 20hp followed the pattern established by its smaller sibling, although interestingly the strengthening fabricated platform was abandoned for the larger car.

Right: Even coachwork was specially designed (and a few prototypes built) for the 20hp, including this 'Ensign' Coach Saloon. Also listed and priced were a Town and Country Saloon, and an Atalanta version. It is believed that all completed cars were scrapped.

Below: Independent suspension for the 20hp was by the André Girling system utilising coils and lever arm dampers. Note also the hydraulically-operated jacking point.

Factory designation	16hp (pre-war)
Date introduced	October 1938
Motor type	6-cyl 4-stroke in-line water-cooled ohv
Dimensions	65 X 100mm = 1991cc
Power/rpm	15.7hp RAC rating
Fuel feed	AC mech pump from rear tank to downdraught Zenith carb
Ignition	battery & coil
Transmission type	4-speed Wilson preselective
Ratios	18.4 10.67 7.24 5.1:1
Final drive ratio	5.1:1 spiral bevel drive
Clutch	Newton centrifugal
Steering	Burman Douglas worm & nut
Suspension	
Front	reverse camber semi-elliptic springs, Luvax double piston dampers
Rear	underslumg semi-ellipic springs, Luvax dampers
Brakes	Girling 4-wheel self-compensating drums, mechanically operated
Wheels	steel discs, bolt-on wires optional
Tyres	5.50 X 17" cross ply
Dimensions	
Wheelbase	9'3"
Track front	4'6"
Track rear	4'6½"
Overall length	14'1½"
Overall width	5'6½"
Height	5'8" (coach saloon)
Unladen weight	27 cwt
Factory coachwork	coach saloon & touring saloon
Variants	per outside coachbuilders eg Charlesworth, Creswell, Salmons & Salmons Tickford
Performance	
Max speed (mph)	74
Fuel consumption (mpg)	25
Number produced	961
Prices	coach saloon & touring saloon £380 (+ optional Philips Motoradio 16gns)
Date last produced	June 1941

THE ARMSTRONG SIDDELEY
DIESEL STATIONARY ENGINES
1945-1959

Alongside their beautifully-crafted motor vehicles, Armstrong Siddeley produced a range of stationary diesel engines. The marque had developed a reputation for mechanical dependability, and while their industrial engines may not have been as silent and inscrutable as the sphinx, they did nothing to tarnish the company name.

Commencement of their production is uncertain, but inspiration for their manufacture came from Chief Engineer Fred Allard, who after the end of World War 2 sought to utilise the now-unwanted space and manpower previously devoted to military production. Worldwide reconstruction created a ready market for small industrial engines, which were quickly designed and built.

The first version was a single cylinder, air-cooled machine evidently intended for light use, developing 10bhp at 1500rpm, and known as the AS1. While the dimensions of their motor-car engines were at that time significantly undersquare, Armstrong Siddeley's direct injection diesel was exactly square at 108X108mm, displacing 988cc. With its 15:1 compression ratio, it was rated at 6bhp at 1000rpm, 7bhp at 1100 rpm, 8bhp at 1200rom, and its maximum output was 10bhp at 1500rpm.

It appears that it was intended for occasional rather than continuous running, since its standard fuel tank held only 3½ gallons of distillate.

The crankshaft was carried in two massive bearings, there was a decompression lever to assist hand-starting, and drive was by pulley from the crankshaft, or at half speed via an extension from the camshaft. A vaned flywheel fan cooled the deeply finned block and alloy cylinder head within metal shrouds. It weighed 530lbs dry, and complete with tools it fitted into a packing case measuring 41 X 34 X 30 inches – ideal for the export drive so aggressively promoted by the post-war British Government.

A promotional leaflet produced for Stokoe Motors of Melbourne, Australia, suggested that the engines may serve as fixed power units for electricity generators, water or sewage pumps, air compressors, concrete mixers, cranes, winches, farm implements or machine-shop power. Many saw service in outback Australia supplying domestic electricity for farmhouses, in the days before widespread connection to reticulated power. Despite their considerable weight the engines were further recommended for portable use as fire pumps, dynamos, compressors, bench saws and arc welders.

From 1949 a twin-cylinder version became available, which was essentially the same engine with a lengthened crankshaft and a second cylinder. Dimensions were identical, displacing 988X2=1976cc, and this AS2 model produced exactly double the power of the single at similar governed engine speeds. The longer crank rode on three large bearings, and its standard fuel tank held five gallons. Like the smaller engine, the crank and bearings were accessible for service through square access doors in the crankcase, while industrial clutches and 2:1 reduction gears were offered for attachment to both engines. In 1950 British Australian Motors of Brisbane, Queensland, Australia catalogued the AS1 and AS2 engines along with the 18hp motor car range – Lancaster, Hurricane, Typhoon, Whitley, Station Coupé and Utility Coupé.

From 1950 the Uxbridge, England firm Diesel Equipment Limited offered single- or three-phase electricity generating sets employing the AS2 engine harnessed to an alternator, complete with switchboard and automatic start. The outfit produced 12 KvA which was adequate for domestic and light industrial power requirements, at least in stand-by mode, and some powered river barges.

The larger engine proved a popular industrial power source in the Netherlands, where the firm of N W Roepers of Nunspeet promoted their use for driving small winnowing machines, heavy-duty pumps and even grain threshers. In England both the singles and twins were popular as power units for canal-boats, in addition to their land-based uses.

In 1955 Armstrong Siddeley enlarged the engine to three cylinders, again simply by lengthening the crankshaft and adding an extra pot and main bearing. Dimensions and compression ratio remained the same, the swept volume was 988X3=2964cc, with four main bearings guaranteeing long crankshaft life. Reportedly there was a very high connectivity between the smallest and largest engines, 65% of whose parts were interchangeable.

At 1500rpm the bigger AS3 engine was rated at 30bhp, but it could run continuously at 1800rpm, when it produced 33bhp. There were two

washable air filters as well as a Tecalemit oil filter, while fuel capacity was increased to 7¾ gallons. It weighed a hefty 970lbs dry, and was clearly intended to supply heavy-duty long-term service chiefly for industrial rather than domestic applications. In that year 3,203 of the single-cylinder version and 12,303 of the twins were produced. There were 322 staff engaged on their manufacture.

Unconfirmed anecdotal evidence suggests that by 1957 Armstrong Siddeley had produced 40,000 diesel stationary engines. They were very highly regarded for their dependability and ease of maintenance – echoing the factory's motor manufacturing philosophy – and many have survived despite long and hard working lives. They deserve a place in the story of Armstrong Siddeley.

ARMSTRONG SIDDELEY ✦

5hp 6hp 7hp 8hp

COMPRESSION **IGNITION ENGINE**

SPECIFICATION

Single Cylinder — Air Cooled — Four Stroke — Cold Starting — Vertical — Compression Ignition Combustion System — Direct Injection.

Bore 4¼ in. Stroke 4¼ in. Capacity 60.3 c. in. 5 b.h.p. 950 r.p.m. 6 b.h.p. 1,000 r.p.m. 7 b.h.p. 1,100 r.p.m. 8 b.h.p. 1,200 r.p.m. Complete with fuel tank, fuel filter, air cleaner and exhaust silencer. The nett weight is 540 lbs.

OVERALL DIMENSIONS

Height	39¾ in.
Width	24 in.
Length	26¾ in.

(With Starting Handle inserted, 37 in.)

Sole Distributors for Victoria and Tasmania:
STOKOE MOTORS PTY. LTD. 265-273 EXHIBITION STREET, MELBOURNE — — — C.1.
Telephone: FJ 4181 and Central 4677 (6 lines).

Air Cooled

Above: Standby electricity generator installation offered by Dutch Armstrong Siddeley dealer, N W Roepers.

Left: Brochure illustration of the AS 1 and AS 2 (twin cylinder) diesel engines. The specifications were identical but with lengthened crankshaft and an extra cylinder for the AS2. Output was exactly doubled.

Far left: Promotional leaflet for the first Armstrong Siddeley diesel stationary engine – the AS1 – produced by Melbourne, Australia dealers, Stokoe Motors. The varying outputs depended on engine revolutions.

A NEW DIESEL
by ARMSTRONG SIDDELEY

FEATURES

AIR COOLING

ACCESSIBILITY

LOW MAINTENANCE COST

RELIABILITY

LOW FUEL CONSUMPTION

Armstrong Siddeley Motors Limited
Coventry · England

20/33HP

Promotional leaflet for the three-cylinder AS3 stationary engine, delivering serious power for permanent and standby electricity generation, power for large boats and similar applications. The dual oil filters can be clearly seen. These engines were built until 1960.

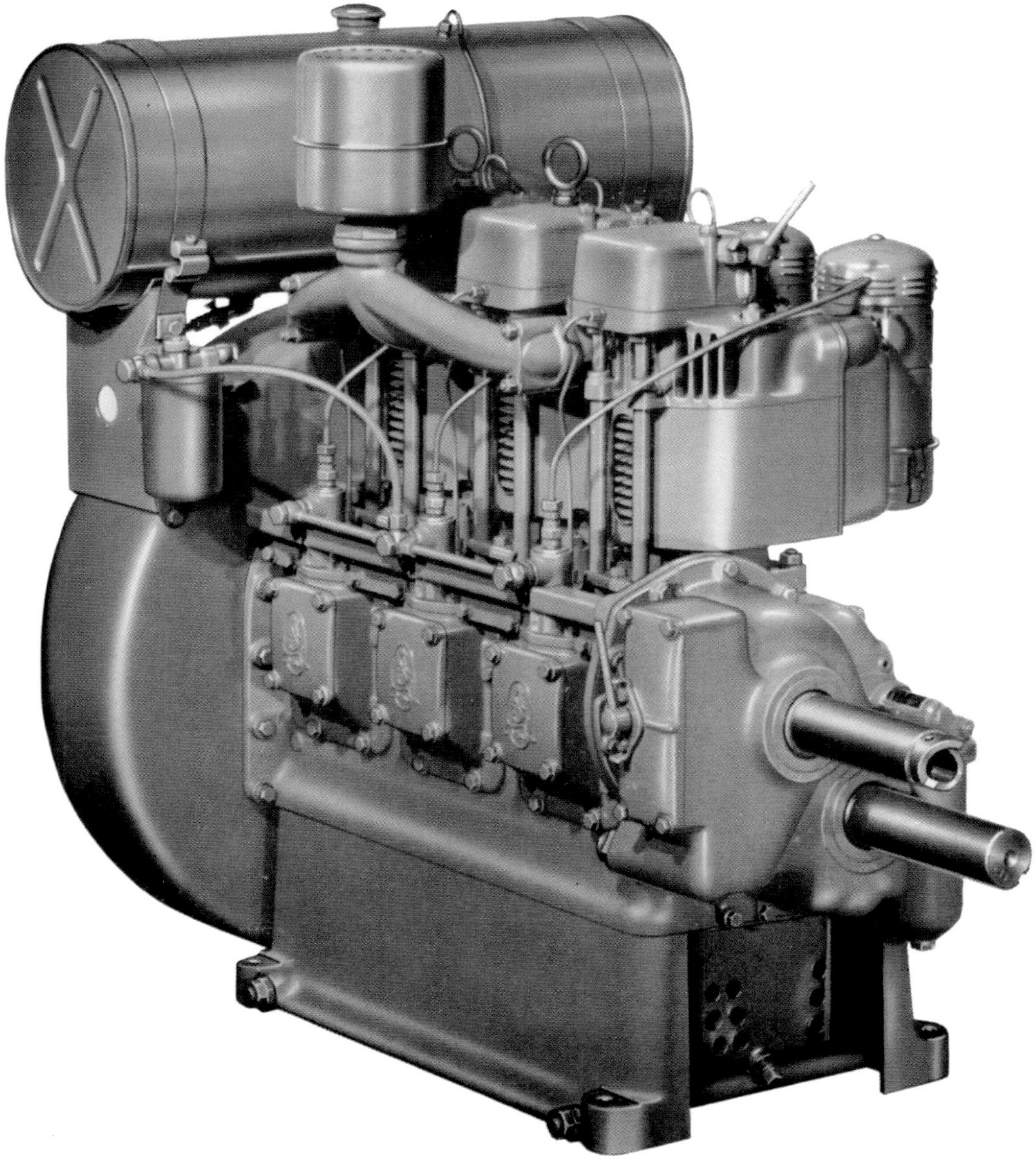

Nearside of the AS3 stationary engine, noting its deeply finned cylinder blocks and separate access for servicing each of the crankshaft's bearings.

THE BENTLEY CONNECTION

Following World War 2, Armstrong Siddeley was the first British motor company to market their new model – the 16hp Hurricane drophead coupé, closely followed by the Mulliner-built Lancaster saloon. Although their engines were similar to the Sixteen so warmly welcomed in 1938, market expectations had moved on, and the post-war Sixteen was seen as lacking power. In everyday use the model could not be expected to top much more than 70mph, or cruise much faster than 50mph, due to its small (1991cc) engine and its low (5.1:1) final drive ratio.

Enter Walter Owen (WO) Bentley, whose sporting cars dominated major motor sport events in the 'twenties, followed by his later designs for the 1930s V12 Lagonda and its 2.6-litre post-war stablemate. Armstrong Siddeley was already toying with its own pushrod overhead valve 2.6-litre alloy six, and very early bored the Sixteen to lift engine capacity to 2.3-litres and 75bhp. But late in 1947, WO was contracted by the company to design what was originally termed a 'sportscar', complete with transmission, chassis and suspension. He established a small consultancy based at Weybridge in Surrey, close to the Brooklands racetrack, taking with him Donald Bastow from his former team. (The Lagonda company was placed on the market earlier in 1947, and was ultimately purchased by David Brown along with Aston Martin, leaving WO and his team free to pursue other endeavours).

What followed were two years of frustration for Bentley's team, as design parameters changed and Armstrong Siddeley management dithered about what sort of animal they had in mind. The company continually pressed for cost controls to maintain final unit price close to that of their existing Sixteens, so neither engine, transmission nor chassis contained many of the Lagonda's costly refinements.

For example, the Lagonda was specified with twin carburettors, while the prototype Armstrong Siddeley had one; the Lagonda employed three chains and nine sprockets to drive its dual overhead camshafts and ancillaries, while the Siddeley prototype used a single chain 4'6" long running around five sprockets. But using the 2.6-litre Lagonda engine as their base, WO's team increased its bores from 78- to 84mm, displacing 2993cc, which was theoretically capable of delivering 125bhp at 5000rpm. WO was also required to investigate, design and report on the reduction of the Lagonda engine's bore size from 78- to 74mm, for a capacity of 2322cc, and also pursue a four-cylinder variant which may serve the lower end of the model range.

Most effort was expended on the 3-litre version, for which calculations showed its power and notional weight would allow it to accelerate from rest to 50mph in 10.8 seconds – a whole 8.1 seconds faster than Armstrong Siddeley's 2.3-litre pushrod prototype. The smaller-capacity 2322cc Lagonda-style motor also theoretically outpaced the factory's 2.3, on paper beating it to 70mph by 13.7 seconds.

WO favoured the Cotal electric planetary type transmission, as fitted to Delage and Delahaye cars before and after the war. His team resolved most if not all the Cotal's inherent design flaws, and such a transmission was installed in the prototype Lagonda 2.6, although replaced by a more conventional four-speed 'box (albeit rear-mounted) in production. A three-speed all-synchromesh unit requested by Armstrong Siddeley was designed, but was probably never built. A four-speed Wilson epicyclic transmission was also considered, with Newton centrifugal clutch or Daimler fluid flywheel, and comparative theoretical performance calculations were supplied to the works.

Initially a chassis frame of roughly similar size to the then-current Sixteen was specified, and only much later did Cyril Siddeley insist that it be enlarged to carry heavier coachwork, when mention was made in Board papers of a 'limousine' rather than a 'sportscar'. The chassis designed by the consultancy was strong yet light, but its manufacture demanded skills then beyond the capacity of established British chassis specialists. Suspension for the Armstrong Siddeley – all independent on the Lagonda 2.6 – was changed to independent front with live rear, chiefly for reasons of cost.

Three of the 3-litre twin overhead camshaft engines were built by Armstrong Siddeley's Experimental Department, and on test achieved the designers' calculated power output of 125bhp at 5000rpm. One was for a time mated to the Cotal-style gearbox and installed in the prototype Sapphire saloon used as personal transport by company executive Selwyn Sharp until 1960, when it had reputedly covered more than 250,000 miles.

A second engine powered a most elegant two-door four-seater cabriolet, its body designed by Swiss coachbuilder Hermann Graber, and used as a mobile test mule. Graber built handsome one-off coupé and convertible bodies for Rover and Bentley (and later Alvis), in addition to their more established European clientele. The dohc engine was installed in an Armstrong Siddeley frame and registered JWK 722 in 1950, and was its only manifestation as anything like a 'sportscar'.

The third engine was used only for bench testing purposes, and all were donated to engineering faculties in British universities when retired from testing. The Graber drophead coupé served as a factory hack until 1960 when it was probably scrapped.

Relations between Armstrong Siddeley and the Bentley consultancy soured markedly when Cyril Siddeley took the reins in 1949, and within months the consultancy's contract was terminated and much of their work was wasted. The factory paid £19,500 for services which did not directly produce the new car originally sought, although the cruciform frame, coil-sprung front suspension and leaf-sprung rear end found form in the Sapphire. The Sapphire's pushrod engine was however designed in-house by Fred Allard, and its concept survived Armstrong Siddeley's demise in the Humber Super Snipe.

Mobile test-bed. This Graber-bodied cabriolet was built on a 16hp chassis and at some stage was powered by the 3-litre Bentley-designed twin overhead camshaft engine.

THE SIXTEEN & EIGHTEEN HP
(POST-WAR) CARS
1945-1954

The post-war Sixteen was announced in *The Autocar* three days after VE Day which ended the hostilities in Europe. A small team developed the new car away from Coventry, confident of demand for the much-modernised vehicle they planned. Messrs Allard, Thornett and Hollister worked from Crackley Hall, at Kenilworth. Their first prototype was tested in 1943, and the new models were named Lancaster and Hurricane in 1944. The company was eager to connect their motor-cars to their wartime aircraft, which a grateful Home market accorded much credit for Nazi Germany's capitulation.

Engine and transmission were inherited in modified form from the pre-war Sixteen. New were hydraulic tappets as pioneered by the Siddeley Special (deleted from the last 800 2.3 litre cars when Lockheed's supply contract expired), plus modifications to crankcase and block, while tuning specialist Harry Weslake recommended altered porting and carburation. The Zenith carburettor was replaced with a downdraught Stromberg, incorporating an automatic choke when manual transmission was specified. Fan and dynamo were belt driven, and a vibration damper was fitted to the Sixteen, although the later 18hp engine was deemed sweet enough without it.

The Wilson preselective transmission was unchanged, but the new car was optionally available with a four-speed manual gearbox built by Borg and Beck. There was synchromesh on the upper three forward ratios, and a central lever. The Hardy-Spicer tailshaft for both versions was open, but varied in length according to wheelbase and the transmission specified, driving proprietary Salisbury 2HA differentials with 5.1:1 final drive ratio. Dunlop steel disc wheels wore 5.50 X 17" tyres for the Home market, or 6.00 X 17" for export, while bolt-on wires were offered for £22.15.7d extra. Interestingly the first catalogue for the Sixteen illustrated the Hurricane with wires, but a modified publication dated May, 1946 showed discs.

The chassis was all-new, comprising side rails cross-braced with a strong cruciform. For the first time on an Armstrong Siddeley, front suspension was independent by Citroën-style adjustable torsion bars, unequal length wishbones and ball-joints, while at the rear underslung semi-elliptic leaf springs rode on Metalastik bushes. A heavy box section connected the rear side-rails to support the tail and the petrol tank, and there was a similarly strong cross-member supporting the radiator and the front of the engine. The complete chassis was

reportedly heavier than its predecessor, but factory figures for the pre-war and post-war Sixteens were identical at 27cwt (1371kg). How much of the later car's weight comprised additional equipment is impossible to define.

Lever-action Girling shock absorbers all round were augmented on early cars with Armstrong DAS8 auxiliary dampers on the front, when rebound control was found to be inadequate on poor roads. Inbuilt mechanical jacks were supplied on all but the utilities. Steering was initially by Burman worm-and-nut, changing to recirculating ball. The column was adjustable for rake via slotted mounting bolts, and all but the utilities provided adjustment for reach. Steering on all versions was exceptionally light and accurate.

There were Girling hydro-mechanical brakes, similar in operation to the early post-war Rover, Bentley, Riley and several other British makes. Front brakes were hydraulically actuated, while the rears were controlled mechanically by rods. When in correct adjustment, the back brakes acted first, avoiding nosedive without requiring compensator mechanisms.

The new car was welcomed enthusiastically by the British motoring press. Montague Tombs wrote in *The Autocar* of December 14, 1945: "In these few words I have attempted to portray the character of a new car which is superb to handle. There is a common saying that a specialised car must really be special in order to sell. This car is genuinely special, and I fancy that any knowledgeable driver who tries it will find the reasons for a display of enthusiasm". Mr Tombs was silent on the matter of performance.

The Autocar tested a 16hp Typhoon 2-door saloon and reported acceleration times in their issue dated February 27, 1948 of 0-30mph in 7.6secs, 0-50mph in 19.5secs, and 0-60mph in 29.7secs. The same journal tested a pre-war Sixteen in 1938, achieving equivalent times of 8.8secs, 17.4secs and 26.9secs, suggesting that the post-war car was slower. Remembering that until 1953 indifferent 'Pool' petrol was all that post-war Britons could buy, poor fuel may explain the later test car's modest performance against the stopwatch.

The Sixteen was however widely regarded as underpowered, however much its road behaviour and equipment impressed testers and buyers alike. By 1947 the works had designed, built and tested their own 2.6 litre pushrod overhead valve alloy engine, but also engaged W O Bentley to design engine, transmission, chassis and suspension for a new car based on the 2.6 litre dohc Lagonda. During the currency of the ultimately futile Bentley consultancy, the factory also enlarged a Sixteen engine to 2309cc, which reached production as the 18hp.

As always the cars were continually upgraded, usually but not only at the changeover from one batch to another. The larger engine,

for example, was for road tax reasons offered for export before becoming available on the Home market. External changes like the early abandonment of rear bumperettes in favour of full-width and eventually pressed steel bumpers, four types of hubcaps, and the adoption of Whitley saloon-style tail treatment for the Hurricane all occurred between batch changes.

All bodies featured the coffin-nosed bonnet suggesting the earliest cars' shovel-shaped radiators, which echoed the form of the (rear radiator) J.D.S.-type Deasy cars. There were horizontal rather than vertical radiator grille bars, shaped front wings incorporating headlamps and, regardless of model, a similarly long and lithe appearance so different from the pre-war verticality typical of British saloons. Standard equipment for all except the utilities included a heater with blower fan and rudimentary demisting facility, carpets throughout, fine polished timber facia and door cappings, and quality leather trim on the seats; cloth trim was occasionally available in the Lancaster and the Typhoon. A valve radio was offered at extra charge, as were fitted suitcases for the Hurricane and the Typhoon (£25.11.1d including purchase tax).

The various bodies offered on the 16/18hp chassis varied significantly, and therefore deserve separate description.

The first was the Hurricane drophead coupé, followed by the Lancaster saloon – its body designed by Armstrong Siddeley but built by Mulliners (Birmingham) due to limited factory space, after the wholesale destruction of the Parkside works by German bombs in 1940 and 1941. The Hurricane used mainly steel and alloy in its construction, with two large rear-hinged doors, chrome-framed windows, individual front seats and a folding hood capable of retention in the coupé-de-ville position or fully lowered. Hydraulic operation of hood and windows was never offered by the factory, but at least one such system was available as an after-market accessory. Latterly the tail assumed the profile of the Whitley saloon, along with its lamps and bumpers. The popular Hurricane was the longest-produced 16/18hp version from May, 1945 to mid 1953, by which time the new Sapphire was in showrooms.

The Lancaster six-light saloon employed much more structural timber, and suffered more than other versions on rough roads. Its coachwork was elegant and spacious, although its luggage compartment was small, and it performed in the same unfussed manner typical of the breed. Top speed in the Sixteen was never much more than 70mph, although a manual gearbox Typhoon was tested at 75mph by *The Autocar* in 1948. In production from 1946, the Lancaster terminated along with supply of their bodies by Mulliners late in 1951, although some were assembled at Parkside in 1952.

From September, 1946 the Typhoon supplied those requiring a stylish two-door sports saloon, by the relatively simple expedient of fitting a fixed roof to the Hurricane. Similar in specification, it used fixed rear side-windows and a framed roof of shaped and padded steel mesh, trimmed with black leatherette reminiscent of the contemporary Riley RM saloons. Relatively short-lived, the Typhoon was deleted from the range late in 1949 before the advent of the Whitley.

In May, 1949 came two variants which raised eyebrows amongst Armstrong Siddeley's carriage-trade clients – the Station Coupé and the Utility Coupé. Both were commercial vehicles built on the 16/18hp frame, to the same high quality as the others. Unique at the time, the Station Coupé had a short loadspace allowing a full four-seater cabin, anticipating the crew cabs of 20 years later. The more conventional Utility Coupé offered more room for loads and less for passengers. Although their mechanical specification was similar to others in the range, changes like the deletion of the adjustable reach steering wheel, replacement of the timber facia and door cappings with painted metal, tough leather trim (leatherette in the rear of the Station Coupé), heavier rear springs and fitment of rubber mats to all floors except the gearbox

Announced within days of VE Day, the Hurricane drophead coupé was once again closely associated with the company's aeronautical activities. The Hawker Siddeley Group purchased Sir John Siddeley's interests in his company, and the Avro Tudor was an early peacetime aircraft built by them. Note the bolt-on wire wheels on this very early Hurricane.

Transportation in the NEW ERA

The Avro Tudor Airliner

The Armstrong Siddeley Car

HAWKER SIDDELEY Group

cover highlighted the cars' workhorse status. The sole 16hp version was used for market assessment in Australia, where ultimately more than 60% of utility production was sold, while the remainder were powered by the 2309cc 18hp engine. Only small numbers were built with the optional preselective transmission, as the huge majority used the four-speed manual gearbox.

The utilities were durable machines, some of which saw service for thirty years and longer, and covered prodigious mileages. More than 1600 examples were produced until mid-1952.

The Whitley four-light saloon was introduced early in 1950, after the production of a handful of the four-light Tempest development prototypes. Differing from that car chiefly in the shape of its rear side-windows, the Whitley showed a handsome new profile with its semi-razor edge styling of roofline and tail. The new design allowed a sizeable luggage compartment without unduly interfering with the interior spaciousness for which the model was renowned.

At the termination of Lancaster production in February, 1952, a six-light Whitley was offered alongside the four-light saloon, although fewer than 300 examples were sold before the last Whitley was built in March, 1954. Roof height was raised on the late four-light saloons, and extra interior space was found by revising depth of the side cushions. With its Whitley-style tail, the Hurricane gained an extra couple of inches of legroom.

The most extravagant versions of the 18hp range were the limousines and landaulettes, built on wheelbases seven inches longer than standard. The company's expected lavish equipment included folding occasional seats, rear heaters and upholstery in leather or cloth. The limousine was heavy at 35cwt (1778kg) for a 2.3 litre engine, not much helped by its use of sixteen-inch wheels. One long chassis was supplied to Messrs Hooper for construction of an opulent two-door drophead coupé body, while the factory built two landaulettes and 122 limousines, all but one of which were fitted with preselective transmissions.

The all-new 3.4 litre Sapphire was announced on October 8, 1952, and was available shortly thereafter. A totally new concept in high performance luxury cars, the new addition immediately outshone the already-dated 18hp, and led to new markets for cars bearing the sphinx mascot.

Below: The handsome form of the early 16hp Hurricane. Note that side flashes, while optional, generally reflected the car's trim colour.

Below right: Early Hurricane cabin, showing the instruments directly ahead of the driver and – in this instance – the synchromesh gearbox rather than the preselective transmission.

Above: Brochure illustration showing just how attractive a Hurricane could be made with contrasting body, hood and flash colours.

Left: Very early prototype Hurricane (note the rear quarter-bumpers, and the triple external door-hinges). Its bolt-on wire wheels were a listed option, but few were specified, and most were fitted to cars destined for the United States.

Above: Announced alongside the Hurricane, the Lancaster was a full six-seater saloon, mainly built by Mulliners of Birmingham. Note the black painted edges to the steel wheels, intended to visually reduce their 17 inch diameter.

Right: The production 16hp Lancaster was a sober, handsome and commodious saloon.

Top right: The company's emphasis was always on interior comfort. The Lancaster offered room to stretch, seated on soft leather and with plenty of air and light.

Far left: The Lancaster's facia, beautifully finished, offered barely sufficient information for the driver, while the cabin's laterally-pleated leather seats offered comfortable accommodation. The floor remained unobstructed when the preselective transmission was specified

Left: Although the Lancaster's body treatment allowed only a shallow luggage compartment, it established the pattern employed by all subsequent Armstrong Siddeleys; the spare wheel and major tools were separately housed, avoiding disturbance of luggage in the event of mishap.

Far left: The 16hp was Armstrong Siddeley's first venture into independent front suspension, after the failed attempt on the still-born pre-war 20hp. Note the ball-jointed system, sprung by torsion bars similar to the Citroën pattern.

Left: Common to all 16hp cars was this compact switch panel, grouping all electrical controls including the starter to the right of the instrument board.

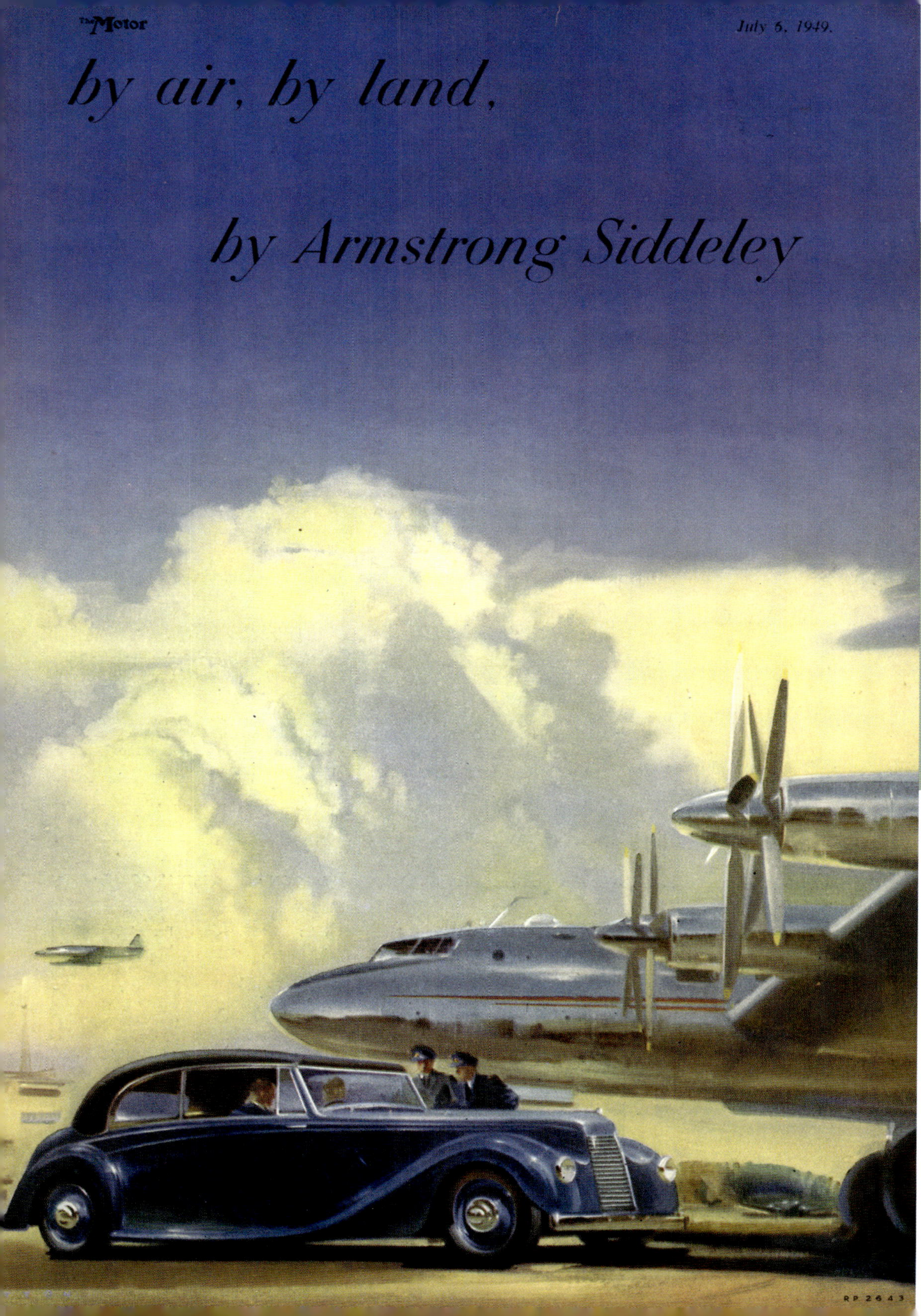
The Motor
July 6, 1949.
by air, by land,
by Armstrong Siddeley
RP 2643

105 WK

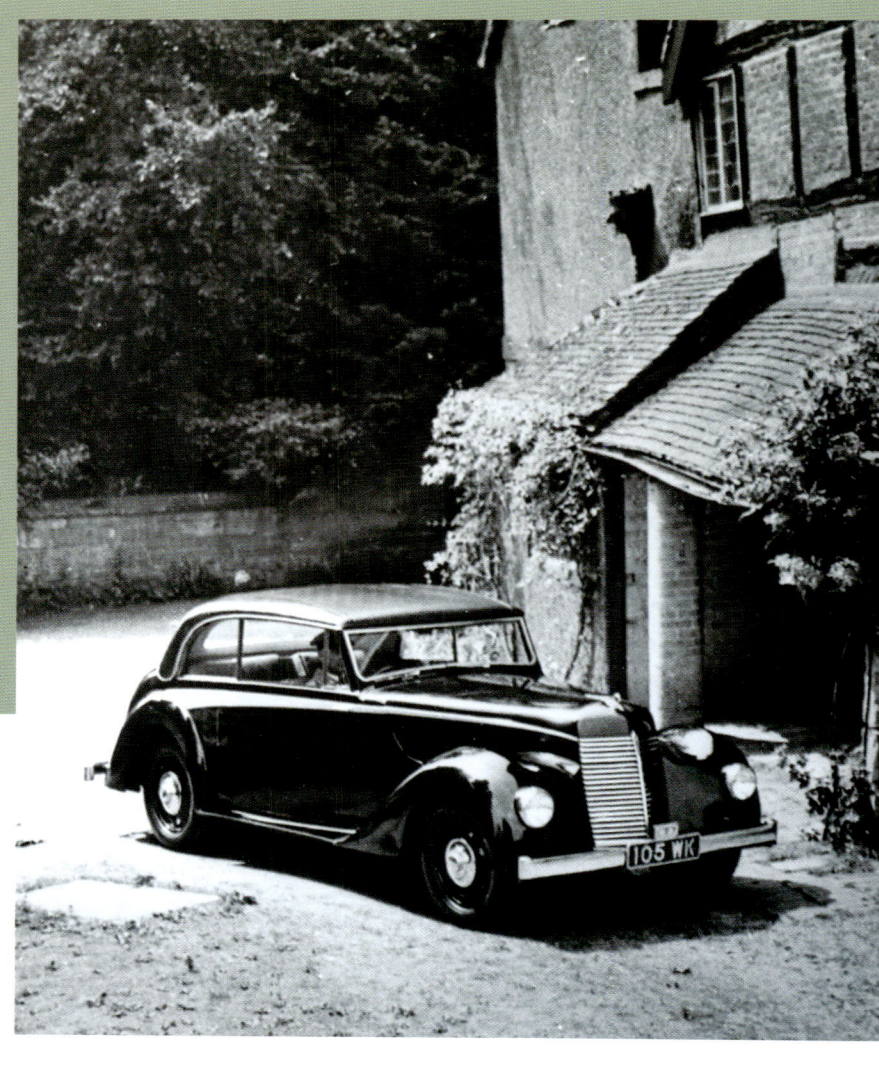

The stylish Typhoon Sports Saloon added a fixed roof to the Hurricane. Standard colour for the leatherette fabric roof covering was black. This body style was almost entirely sold with the 16hp engine, although a few 18hp versions were built before production ended in 1949.

Opposite page: Early advertising for the new Typhoon model continued the attachment to the company's experience in aeronautics. This very attractive image dates from 1946.

The Whitley

WHITLEY · The Cars of Character

The Cars of Character · WHITLEY

THE AUTOCAR, APRIL 4, 1952

ASM 18

ARMSTRONG SIDDELEY

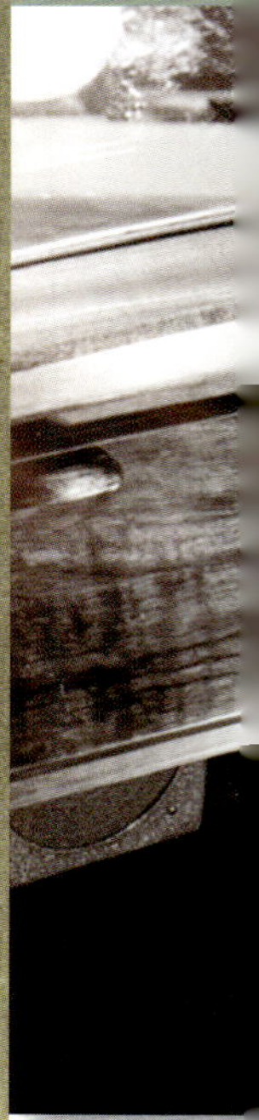

Left: The new 18hp Whitley saloon was built in-house by Armstrong Siddeley, and augmented rather than replaced the existing Lancaster saloon. Its attractive four-light semi-razor-edge styling offered spacious passenger accommodation and improved luggage space.

Far left: Commencement of the 18hp engine saw this revised dashboard treatment, which was applied across the range except for the utilities. In this instance an optional radio is fitted.

Above: The larger-engined Lancaster was identifiable by fewer grille bars, and the revised bonnet arrangement, common to all body styles.

Right: The production 18hp Hurricane showed external changes from the 16hp similar to the Lancaster – chiefly in terms of number and style of radiator grille bars, and alligator bonnet.

The last Hurricanes used Whitley-style rear treatment, and the Whitley's pressed steel bumpers.

Above: The introduction of the six-light Whitley coincided with the phasing out of the Lancaster. At the same time the roof height of the four-light Whitley was raised for improved passenger accommodation.

Above right: The carriage trade was served by the introduction of the long-wheelbase limousine, lavishly appointed but still powered by the 75bhp 2.3-litre engine.

Opposite page: The long wheelbase car was also available as a landaulette, this example famously ordered for the Sultan of Zanzibar.

AMPLE ACCOMMODATION FOR FOUR OR FIVE

A SOURCE OF PRIDE IN ANY SETTING

Station Coupé

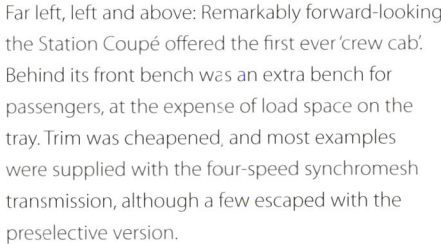

Far left, left and above: Remarkably forward-looking, the Station Coupé offered the first ever 'crew cab'. Behind its front bench was an extra bench for passengers, at the expense of load space on the tray. Trim was cheapened, and most examples were supplied with the four-speed synchromesh transmission, although a few escaped with the preselective version.

Above: For those serious about load-space, the company also offered the Utility Coupé, built to the same specification but with one bench seat.

Coachbuilder Pennock of The Hague built six drophead coupé bodies on the 18hp chassis. They were mechanically identical, and bodily very similar, to the factory's Hurricane.
Upper: Drawing of Pennock cabriolet with hood lowered, by John Bull.
Lower: brochure illustration of the car with hood raised.

Left: The 1952 range of Armstrong Siddeley vehicles (not including any long wheelbase cars) as shown by Southern Motors, Adelaide, Australia.

Right: This one-off fixed head coupe was built on the 18hp chassis by Italian coachbuilder Carrozzeria Ghia, and was exhibited at the Turin Salon in 1952. It bore strong resemblance to designs on Bentley chassis by Pininfarina and Facel.

Below: Coachbuilder Hooper built one only drophead coupé on the long 18hp wheelbase. The car survives. Drawing by John Bull.

	16hp	18hp
Factory designation	16hp	18hp
Date introduced	May 1945	1949 (export only initially)
Motor type	6-cyl 4-stroke in-line ohv (hydraulic tappets)	last 800 cars solid tappets
Dimensions	65 X 100mm=1991cc	70 X 100mm=2309cc
Power/rpm	70bhp @ 4200rpm	75bhp @ 4200rpm
Fuel feed	Stromberg downdraught DAA36 carb, with mechanical fuel pump	
Ignition	battery & Lucas coil	same
Transmission type	optional 4-speed synchromesh (synchro 2-3-4), or Wilson preselective	
Ratios	synchro: 3.42 2.135 1.419 1:1 Rev 2.982 Wilson: 3.6 2.89 1.416 1:1 Rev 4.469	
Final drive	Salisbury 2HA, 5.1:1 all models including long wheelbase	
Clutch	synchro: Borg & Beck 9" single dry plate Wilson: 8½" Newton dry centrifugal	
Steering	Burman worm & nut, but from late 16hp recirculating ball	
Suspension		
Front	independent by torsion bars, ball-joints, lever-action Lucas Girling PV6 dampers, plus later auxiliary Armstrong DASS lever action dampers (not for utilities)	
Rear	semi-elliptic springs mounted in Metalastik bushes, number of leaves varied according to body weight, with Girling lever action dampers	
Brakes	standard wheelbase: Girling hydro-mechanical (front self-adjusting hydraulic, rear mechanical), 12" drums with one leading and one trailing shoe.	
	long wheelbase: Lockheed all-hydraulic system with 12" drums, 2 leading shoes on front, one leading and one trailing shoe at rear	
Wheels	3.25" 17" steel discs standard; 17" bolt-on wire wheels optional but fitted chiefly to Hurricanes for export; long wheelbase 16" steel discs	
Tyres	5:50 X 17 cross ply, 6.00 X 17 for export, (long wheelbase 6.00 X 16" cross ply)	
Dimensions		
Wheelbase	9'7"	same, (long wheelbase 10'2")
Track front	4'6"	same, (long wheelbase 4'6 5/8")
Track rear	4'6½"	same, (long wheelbase 4'9")
Overall length	Hurricane/Typhoon 15'6" Lancaster 15'7½" Whitley/Station Coupé/Coupé Utility 15'5" Limousine/Landaulette 16'3"	
Overall width	5'8"	same, (long wheelbase 5'10")
Height	Lancaster 5'2" Hurricane (hood erect)/Typhoon 5'1" Whitley 5'3" Limousine/Landaulette 5'7½"	
Unladen weight	passenger cars 29-30cwt, utilities 28cwt, long wheelbase 35¼ cwt	
Factory coachwork	Lancaster 6-light saloon; Hurricane drophead coupé; Typhoon sports saloon; Tempest 4-light saloon; Whitley 4-light and six-light saloons; Station Coupé; Coupé Utility; limousine; landaulette	
Variants	Coachbuilt versions, most notably six cabriolets built by Pennock of The Hague, 1 long wheelbase drophead coupé by Hooper, 1 fixed head coupé by Ghia	
Performance		
Max speed (mph)	75	80
Fuel consumption (mpg)	18-21	23-25
Number produced	Lancaster 3597 Hurricane 2606 Typhoon 1701 Tempest 6 Whitley 4-light 2303 Whitley 6-light 279 limousine 122 (inc landaulette 2) ***	
Prices (incl purchase tax)	1948-1950: Lanc/Typh £1246.11.8 Lanc/Whit£1272.2.9 Limo £1757.13.11	
	1953: Hurricane, Whitley 4-lt & 6-lt £1557.1.1	
Date last produced		
	*** subject to dispute. Numbers researched by Robert Penn Bradly used for these figures	

THE JET-PROPELLED WHITLEY

Many motor manufacturers built complete aircraft, aero engines and/or components during World War 2. At war's end, all scrabbled to redirect staff and manufacturing capacity toward alternative production, applying the new technologies learned during wartime.

Under its new ownership, Armstrong Siddeley was deeply involved in aircraft manufacture, and explored the use of gas turbine engines in motor-cars. Their Experimental Department began work on a small turbine in August, 1949, and lodged a complete specification with the British Patents Office on 21st September, 1950. Their application was for a patent over "A gas turbine unit, particularly for driving motor vehicles".

The design was accepted on 3rd April, 1952, and was awarded Patent Number 145,977. The drawing accompanying the specifications shows the outline of a Whitley saloon, with a box aft of the engine compartment, and the comment that it "may include a clutch and a reversing gear", although by what means is not specified.

Armstrong Siddeley was not alone in exploring the use of jet engines for automotive propulsion at that time. First to build and test such a car was the British Rover company, whose modified P4 roadster used a rear-mounted turbine producing 230bhp at 26,000rpm, and reached 151.98mph on the Jabbekke motorway in Belgium in June, 1952.

From 1952, Austin installed a turbine in a modified Sheerline saloon, which produced a relatively modest 125bhp at 23,000rpm, and drove the big car at about 70mph; but only if you could feed it jet fuel at the rate of 4.5mpg.

On the Continent, Fiat built its attractive Turbina in 1954, which produced 220bhp at 22,000rpm, and was tested at 155mph. Renault's Étoile Filante (Shooting Star) was even more powerful, produced 270bhp at 28,000rpm and reached a speed of 192.5mph on Bonneville Salt Flats in Utah, USA.

Stateside, Chrysler tried a turbine in a 1953 Plymouth sedan, while from 1953 to 1959 General Motors installed turbines in 'dream' cars, about which there is little reliable performance data despite plenty of hype.

The company that started it all, Rover, persisted with their smart T3 coupé of 1956, which featured four-wheel drive and four-wheel inboard disc brakes. Their later T5 was clothed in bodywork which anticipated the P6-2000 series, and appeared to point toward production. In 1963, Rover collaborated with BRM to enter the LeMans 24-hour race, but in demonstration mode only, with a turbine-powered car allowed double the usual fuel allocation. The car would have placed eighth had it been competing.

At this distance in time we can only speculate on just how serious was Armstrong Siddeley's interest in powering a car by turbine. As demonstrated by Austin and by Rover-BRM, the Achilles heel of all automotive gas turbine engines is their thirst for fuel, and their dislike of constant acceleration and braking; used in aircraft, they much prefer a constant engine speed.

Describing the acceleration of the Sapphire 346 limousine in late 1956, one particular road-tester said "She gathers up her skirts and sweeps away like an angry Duchess". It remains intriguing to wonder how much more angrily a production Siddeley may have 'swept away' with a jet engine under her skirts.

" No, same old car . . . new engine . . ."

CHAPTER XI

THE SAPPHIRE 346

1952-1958

The Bentley consultancy may have ended in acrimony and frustration for WO and his team, but many of their design parameters survived in the spectacular Armstrong Siddeley Sapphire, introduced in October, 1952.

The consultancy's chassis, and independent front suspension by wishbones and coils, formed the foundation of Armstrong Siddeley's high-speed express, departing so dramatically from its immediate predecessors. The frame was stronger than the 16/18hp version, comprising deep channel sections – massively strengthened with cross bracing – and a removable front sub-frame. Side rails tapered front and rear to give the chassis crumple resistance years ahead of its time, providing protection for occupants in the event of major impact. The front suspension, by coil springs within unequal length and rearward trailing wishbones and enclosed Girling shock absorbers, gave very modern independent springing, supported by a live rear axle on conventional leaf springs – as requested by the company from the Bentley consultancy. Thoughtfully the coil spring on the driver's side was longer than the other, giving an even stance when regularly carrying only the driver. There were anti-roll bars front and rear

(although the rear bar was deleted from the last of the Mark 2 cars), and the complete chassis weighed only 62lbs more than the 18hp.

Bentley's twin overhead camshaft 3-litre engine was replaced by an in-house design by Fred Allard – designer of the fabled Siddeley Special engine – again departing markedly from its predecessors. The in-line six comprised a strong cast iron block-cum-crankcase, a forged and counterbalanced crankshaft made of carbon steel with four large main bearings, and square bore/stroke dimensions of 90mm displacing 3435cc – cylinders were bored direct into the block without separate liners.

To achieve the hemispherical combustion chambers deemed essential by the consultancy, Allard used a single camshaft mounted high in the block, driving pushrods to separate rocker shafts for inlet and exhaust valves. This system allowed angled valves and centrally located spark-plugs without the complication of dual camshafts, and was the principal contributor to the Sapphire's high power output. Such arrangements were not new, since the BMW 328 engine used a single camshaft and dual rocker shafts (but with short additional cross-pushrods) from 1936.

The Sapphire's original 6.5:1 compression ratio and single Stromberg DAV36 downdraught carburettor produced 120bhp at 4200rpm. In production compression was lifted to 7:1 producing 125bhp at 4700rpm; when optionally supplied with twin Stromberg DAA36 carbs, power lifted to 150bhp at 5000rpm. In this latter form the Sapphire reached 50mph in 8.9 seconds, faster than the twin-cam twin-carb Mark VII Jaguar which took 9.8 seconds for the same sprint. Top speeds of the competing cars were almost identical. At the desirable 2500 ft/minute piston speed, the new 'square' motor drove the Sapphire in top gear at 86mph, making it a true motorway stormer with performance surpassing many contemporary sports cars.

Two optional transmissions were offered initially – a four speed all-synchromesh 'box with column-mounted change, or the Wilson epicyclic preselector unit with electric selection. The synchromesh gearbox was bought in from the Rootes Group, which used identical units in the Mark IV Humber Super Snipe from 1954 to 1956. (The Bentley consultancy designed and built a three-speed all synchromesh gearbox for the ill-fated 3-litre car, which may have formed the basis for the similar unit fitted to Humber Hawks and Super Snipes from 1957).

Bentley had urged Armstrong Siddeley to consider a modified version of the Cotal electric epicyclic gearbox for the 3-litre car. The original Cotal design used a miniature gate attached to the steering column, with four positions. A master control lever on the floor selected forward or reverse drive, after which theoretically one could drive as fast in reverse as in forward, using all four ratios. The consultancy deleted the master lever in favour of a separate reverse gear, all ratios controlled electrically from a five-position column-mounted switch. The Sapphire's 'preselectric' system used a similar electric switch, with solenoid-activated selectors mounted on the side of the Wilson gearbox. As previously there was a centrifugal plate clutch and four forward ratios.

An open tailshaft with a centre support bearing drove through a Salisbury 2HA (later 4HA) differential similar to that of the late 18hp cars, but with a final drive ratio of 4.09:1. Some buyers specified an alternate 3.77:1 ratio, as was later fitted to the Star Sapphire. Brakes were unboosted hydraulic Girling 11" drums all round, with twin leading shoes at the front, and steering was by Burman recirculating ball mechanism.

The steel body was all-new, designed and built in-house. Offered optionally in six-light and four-light forms at similar prices, it combined the grace of flowing wing-lines with enough tradition to satisfy the marque's established clientele, including sufficient rear head-room to allow passengers to wear hats. Both styles swung front and rear doors from the centre pillars, cabins were light and airy – especially in the more numerous six-light version – and excellent vision was afforded by very slender windscreen pillars, and a high seating position. Fine leather was used for all seat facings, with deeply upholstered benches front and rear.

There was minimal use of structural timber, even though polished walnut was used decoratively for facia and door cappings. The luggage compartment – variously trimmed in a figured board or carpet – provided ample space for touring needs, with separate housing for the spare wheel and major tools; hand tools occupied a small lined tray.

Not surprisingly this radical departure from the company's traditions drew comment from the motoring press, *The Motor* in its October 8, 1952 announcement of the new model saying: "Any entirely new model from the Armstrong Siddeley factory would command special attention by reason of the company's reputation for quality and finish – a reputation which, not unnaturally perhaps, seems common to car-manufacturing concerns with aircraft associations. In the case, however, of the new Armstrong Siddeley Sapphire, there are two other notable reasons for this new model having special claim to attention.

"One is that, with its unusual 3.4-litre, six-cylinder 'square' engine developing 120bhp and its relatively light dry weight of 31cwt (3149kg), it marks the entry of Armstrong Siddeley Motors Ltd, into the high-performance class, with a potential maximum speed very well in excess of 90mph". In fact on test their twin-carburettor synchromesh

Below right: This very early production Sapphire displays the unadorned elegance of the car's basic form, and its appeal in contrasting shades of paint colour.

Opposite page: One of the few colour advertisements for the very colourful Sapphire, especially when painted in two tones. This appeared in *The Autocar* of 7th May, 1954.

four-light Sapphire recorded a maximum speed of 100.8mph , 0-50mph in 8.9 seconds, and speeds on the indirects of 33, 50 and 75mph. They commented: "We expected this car to perform well, but were a little surprised when, for example, the 0-60mph acceleration time proved to be better than anything which we have recorded since the war in a five-six seater saloon car... this car seems happy to cruise indefinitely at 80mph on modern continental motor roads". Testers noted that individual front seats were available for an extra £25, the preselectric gearbox for £30 more than the synchromesh version, while a single carburettor lopped £25 from the £1757.15.10 price. This was incidentally around £500 more expensive than the last Whitley, emphasising that the new car was competing in a whole new market sector.

The Sapphire was an immediate market hit, including many shipped to America. Some 1693 cars were built in the first full production year (1953). The carriage trade was not forgotten, since from September, 1952 it was the company's intention to market a long wheelbase version alongside the saloon. Five limousines were built by William Vincent Ltd of Reading, a provincial coachbuilder which clothed its first Rolls-Royce in 1906. Although anticipating the basic shape of the factory-built limousine – not introduced until March, 1955 – the Vincent cars were identified by their retention of the semaphore trafficators, windscreen and ribbed opaque tail lamp lenses of the early saloons. Production cars shared the blinkers and red tail lamp lenses of the Mark 2 cars, with a taller windscreen and re-profiled rear roof panel to maintain the proportions of the saloon, while increasing head-room and improving driver vision.

The limousines featured lavish interior accommodation, with rear compartments in fine leather or West-of-England cloth trim, extra courtesy lamps, separate heating system and clock, grab-handles and rope door-pulls. Although running a slightly shorter final drive ratio (4.45 vs 4.09:1), the rolling radius of larger section 7.00 X 16 tyres produced overall gearing very close to that of the saloon.

The huge majority of both short and long chassis were bodied by the works, but some were converted into Countryman saloons by Harold Radford (Coachbuilders) Ltd of London, who installed fully reclining front seats, picnic tables, picnic sets and folding occasional seats. Similar fittings produced Countryman versions of the period Rolls-Royce and Bentley models. On the long chassis were built three ambulances, one vast shooting brake, one long mobile display utility and 14 hearses.

Although as before the cars' specifications were continually upgraded, from August, 1954 a Mark 2 version incorporated a raft of subtle changes, and became known as the Sapphire 346 to separate it in the market from its Sapphire 236/234 siblings. Externally identifiable mainly by its blinking trafficators and its red tail lamps, underneath there were major changes.

The braking system was all-new, with 12" ribbed drums replacing the 11" drums on the earlier cars, plus the routine fitment of a Clayton

Double life of a *Sapphire*

The Autocar, 7 May 1954

FOR HIM

Good looks *plus* smooth, silent, surging acceleration. 0—50 m.p.h. through the gears in 8.9 seconds! A terrific 3rd to speed you up to 75 m.p.h. A top gear that will reach around the 100 mark or cruise happily in the seventies with the twin-carburetter 150 b.h.p. engine scarcely purring.

Yet for all its tremendous power, the Sapphire will give you 22 miles per gallon. Centrifugal clutch and pre-selectric gears glide you gently at the slowest crawl when needs must. Special stabilizers prevent all roll when cornering. Braking matches acceleration.

In every way the Sapphire is worthy of its engine —built side by side with the famous Sapphire Jets which power the world's finest aircraft: the Gloster Javelin, the Hawker Hunter, the Vulcan, the Victor, and in the U.S.A., the B.57, the F.J.3 Fury, and the Republic Thunderstreak.

FOR HER

Each time you see the Sapphire, you admire the sweeping lines and gemlike perfection a little more. Each time you experience its air of authority and dignity you secretly hug yourself a little tighter. But perhaps most of all you delight in the sheer luxury of the Sapphire's interior. Walnut panelling. Deep cushion seating. Deep pile carpets. An easy step in and out. Extra wide flat floor. Front seat adjustable at a finger touch. Clear all round view.

And (if you ever get the chance) how pleasant to drive the Sapphire. Responsive, docile. As easy to handle as a car half its size and weight.

Write to Armstrong Siddeley Motors Ltd., Coventry, for fully descriptive catalogue.

The amazing ARMSTRONG SIDDELEY SAPPHIRE

Single carburetter, synchro gears **£1,722** *(including tax). Twin carburetter and pre-selectric gearbox optional extras.*

MEMBER OF THE HAWKER SIDDELEY GROUP

Below right: Although
evidently posed, this
photograph emphasises the
extent to which the Sapphire
body shell was hand-finished.

Opposite page: An
advertisement dating
from October 10, 1952,
and thought to show the
prototype 4-light Sapphire
saloon. At this time the car
was still known as the 340.

Dewandre vacuum booster. Front brakes used trailing rather than leading shoes, and the new system proved itself better able to cope with sustained high speed motorway driving. Outer wishbones in the front suspension were supported on Metalastik bushes requiring no lubrication.

Buyers could then specify at extra cost optional equipment including electrically-controlled window lifts, Telaflo rear dampers adjustable for firmness from the driver's seat, and the first and only application of variable assistance power steering. This latter equipment offered via quadrant control on the dashboard the option of no assistance, full assistance or anything in between. This was a welcome addition to the handling options of a heavy motor-car. Since it was seemingly reliable in long service, it remains a mystery why it was not used on other large luxury vehicles.

A fully automatic four-speed transmission – built by Rolls-Royce under licence from General Motors – was added to the synchromesh and preselectric options late in 1954. Identical to the 'box used in the contemporary Rolls-Royce Silver Cloud and Bentley S-series, the Hydra-Matic offered four forward ratios controlled by a steering-column mounted lever. Mated to the engine by a fluid coupling but omitting a torque-converter, it produced automatic shifts with minimal power loss but considerable roughness. Ratios of the indirects were short for the engine's power, and provided maxima of only 12, 28 and 58mph. Despite engines of 4.9 litres, the Rolls-Royce and Bentley only reached 63mph in third, although their maximum in fourth was well over the hundred. Performance of the automatic Sapphire was markedly slower than for those equipped with the alternative gearboxes, 0-50mph taking 10.9 seconds on a twin carburettor automatic car (compared to 8.9 seconds for a synchromesh version), although the 101mph maximum was similar.

Almost all standard-wheelbase Mark 2 cars were sold as six-light saloons, although 25 were built in four-light form. Ever willing to fill market niches, the company built 45 Sapphire pick-ups for use in the Middle East by an oil company, utilising the standard chassis but

with drastically simplified trim and equipment, uprated suspension and synchromesh transmissions. Production was not continued beyond the initial contract.

Sales reached a low ebb of just 126 cars in 1957, lifting to 386 from January to September in the following year, when the extensively revised Star Sapphire was released. The 346 limousine continued in production until the Star version was released in January, 1960. Total production of Mark 1 and Mark 2 Sapphires was 7680 vehicles in six years (averaging 1097 per annum), comparing more than favourably with Bentley's S-type which sold just 3107 (or an average of 621 per annum) between 1955 and 1959. The Mark 2 Sapphire equalled the Bentley's top speed, boasted greater interior and luggage space, consumed about 20% less fuel, and cost less than one third of its purchase price.

THE NEW *Sapphire*

NORWICH:
Howes & Sons Ltd., Chapel Field

NOTTINGHAM:
T. Forbes Ltd., Castle Boulevard

PETERBOROUGH:
G. K. Hunter Ltd., Wentworth Street

PLYMOUTH:
Allens of Plymouth, Tavistock Road

READING:
Vincents of Reading, Station Square

SHEFFIELD, 2:
Essam & Hewson Ltd., London Road

SHREWSBURY:
Shuker & Son Ltd., Pride Hill

SOUTHAMPTON:
Wadham Bros. Ltd., Bannister Road

HOVE, 2:
A. S. Tilley Ltd., Davigdor Road

WOLVERHAMPTON:
B. P. Littleford Ltd., Albany Road

ARMSTRONG SIDDELEY

Three optional transmissions were available during the life of the Sapphire. The synchromesh Humber gearbox with conventional clutch; the Wilson preselective gearbox with centrifugal Newton clutch and electric selection from the tiny gate to the left of the steering wheel; and (for the Mark II cars from late 1955) the General Motors Hydramatic four-speed automatic.

Brochure image showing the four-light saloon in a single paint colour. The large majority were finished in duo tones, and while there was an extensive colour chart, paint colour was to customer choice.

The most notable external features of the Mark II cars were its blinking trafficators, its slightly more even profile stance, and its stone-guards on the rear wings. Underneath there were far more significant changes.

Sapphire 346 Limousine

CAN ALSO BE

FITTED WITH

CONTROLLED

POWER STEERING

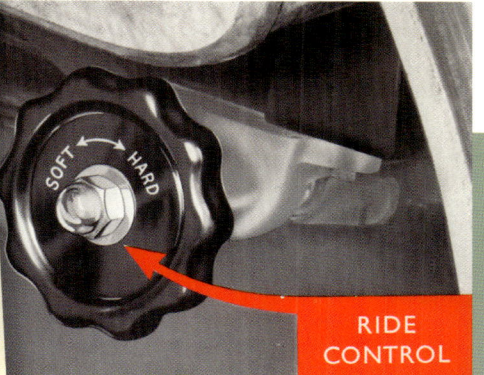

RIDE CONTROL

The New

Sapphire 234 and 236

The two sensational new smaller sisters of the Sapphire each have special points of interest. The 236 has the unique MANUMATIC no clutch pedal control. The 234 with synchromesh gearbox has 100 m.p.h. performance. Both are full 5-seater saloons with 13½ cu. ft. luggage boots and 30 m.p.g. performance

ARMSTRONG SIDDELEY MOTORS LIMITED · COVENTRY

Member of the Hawker Siddeley Group

POWER OPERATED WINDOWS

AN ADVANCE IN COMFORT AND SAFETY

CONTROLLED

POWER STEERING

ON THE

Sapphire 346

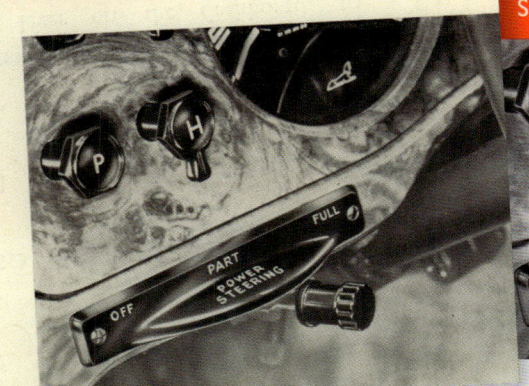

POWER STEERING

Responding to an order from a Middle East oil company, Armstrong Siddeley built 45 of these detuned and stripped Sapphire pick-ups. On lower compression motors they delivered 100bhp, were all fitted with synchromesh transmissions and minimal external and interior trim. The available load-space was surprisingly small, given that they were built on the standard Sapphire wheelbase.

218

Above left and above: After construction of prototypes by Vincent of Reading, the long wheelbase Sapphire limousine was introduced in Mark II guise in 1958. It retained the handsome proportions of the saloon by subtle enlargement and reprofiling of many of its panels.

Left: Appleyard-Rippon Ltd of Leeds built this estate car on a Mark II Sapphire chassis. It was destined to remain a one-off. Schemes were prepared for such bodies by at least one other coachbuilder, but none reached production.

The elegant Sapphire was ideally suited to the funerary trade, and 14 hearses were built on the long frame. Here a hearse coachbuilt by Woodall Nicholson leads three long wheelbase limousines serving as mourning coaches. The hearse survives.

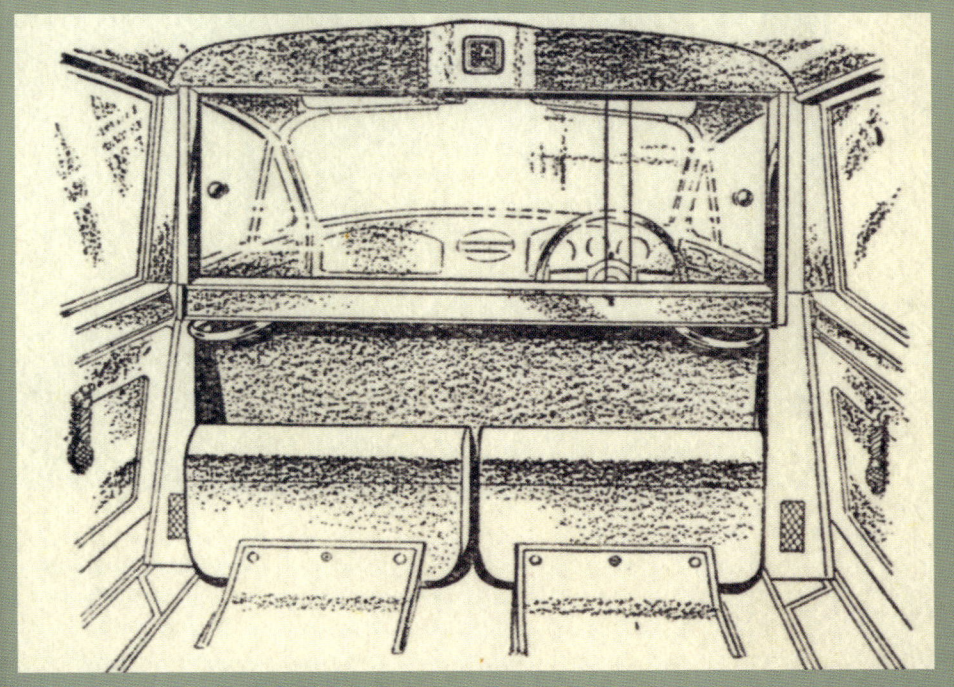

Above: View from the throne. Note the sliding glass partition, extra clock, and ventilation outlets on each side of the partition.

Left: The Sapphire limousine was true to the company's traditions, with lavish appointments to the rear passenger compartment. Note the floor rug, the folding occasional seats, the West of England cloth trim, tasselated door-pulls, and the heater controls in the passenger's armrest.

236 MANUMATIC

Which is your *Sapphire?*

236 Manumatic. Most compact, most economical, most refinement for the price plus
the ease of two-pedal driving and 30 m.p.g.
234 Synchromesh, its twin. Most verve - and over the 100 mark in top.
346 Limousine seven-seater. Most luxury and space at the price.
346 Automatic. Most brilliant 100 m.p.h. performance. No-clutch control and
22 m.p.g. on the open road. The only car in the world with controlled power steering.
Sapphire brilliance springs from the engineering 'know-how' behind the
Sapphire jet aero engine - power unit for many
of the world's fastest aircraft.

346 LIMOUSINE

346 AUTOMATIC

Sapphire 236 Manumatic
£1469.17.0 (Incl.£490.17.0 P.T.)
Sapphire 236 Synchromesh
£1439.17.0 (Incl.£480.17.0 P.T.)
Sapphire 234 Synchromesh
£1411.7.0 (Incl.£471.7.0 P.T.)
Sapphire 346 Automatic £2107.7.0 (Incl. £703.7.0 P.T.)
Sapphire 346 Limousine £2866.7.0 (Incl. £956.7.0 P.T.)
Write to
ARMSTRONG SIDDELEY MOTORS LTD *Coventry, for Catalogue 346, 236 or 234*
► ◄ M E M B E R   O F   T H E   H A W K E R   S I D D E L E Y   G R O U P ► ◄

This June, 1958 advertisement in *The Motor* shows
that Armstrong Siddeley was covering three or four
market sectors with its limited range of motor vehicles.
The breadth of specifications possible by exercising
the factory's options scheme was wide, yet its prices
compared to their opposition were reasonable.

	Sapphire	Sapphire 346 Mark II	Sapphire 346 limousine
Factory designation	Sapphire	Sapphire 346 Mark II	Sapphire 346 limousine
Date introduced	Olympia Motor Show, October 1952	August 1954	1955
Motor type	6-cyl 4-stroke in-line water-cooled ohv	same	same
Dimensions	90 X 90mm = 3435cc	same	same
Power/rpm	(single carb) 125bhp @ 4400rpm (pick-up 100bhp)	same	same
	(optional twin carb) 150bhp @ 5000rpm	same	same
Fuel feed	mech pump from rear tank to Stromberg carb(s)	same	same
Ignition	battery & coil, automatic advance,		
Transmission type	4-spd & Rev all-synchro	same	same
	4-spd & Rev electrically-controlled Wilson	same	same
		same plus option of Hydramatic 4-spd & Rev auto	
Ratios	(synchro) 12.8 8.55 5.8 4.091 Rev 13.54		(synchro) 13.93 9.3 6.32 4.451 Rev 14.73
	(preselective) 13.9 8.15 5.56 4.091 Rev 19.47	(auto) 15.62 10.77 5.93 4.091 Rev 17.6	(preselective) 15.13 8.87 6.05 4.451 Rev 21.18
			(auto) 17 11.72 6.45 4.451 Rev 19.15
Final drive ratio	4.091:1 (rare option of 3.77:1)	same	4.451:1
Clutch	(synchro) 10" Borg & Beck dry plate	same	same
	(preselective) Newton centrifugal	(auto) fluid coupling	same
Steering	Burman recirculating ball	same, variable power assistance optional	same
Suspension			
Front	independent coils & wishbones, telescopic dampers	same	same
Rear	semi-elliptic springs, telescopic dampers	same, Telaflo adjustable dampers optional	same
Brakes	4-whl 11" drums twin leading shoes on front	12" drums, 1 lead 1 trailing shoe, vacuum booster	same, Girling hydraulic system
Wheels	Dunlop steel disc	same	same
Tyres	6.50 X 16" cross ply	6.70 X 16" cross ply	7.00 X 16" cross ply
Dimensions			
Wheelbase	9'6"	same	11'1"
Track front	4'8 5/8"	same	same
Track rear	4'9½"	same	same
Overall length	16'1"	same	17'8"
Overall width	6'0"	same	same
Height	5'5½"	same	5'8½"
Unladen weight	32½ cwt	34¼ cwt	36 cwt
Factory coachwork	4-lt & 6-lt saloons	same	7-seater 4-dr limousine
Variants	per outside coachbuilders, Minerva cabriolet	same, Appleyard estate car, 45 oil company pick-ups	coachbuilt hearses, 1 lwb shooting brake & utility
Performance			
Max speed (mph)	(single carb) 94 (twin carb) 100	(single carb) 97 (twin carb) 101	
Fuel consumption (mpg)	18-22	16.8	
Number produced	3724	3956	379
Prices	£1573.12.6 including Purchase Tax	£1722 incl PT	synchro £2866.7.0 auto £3149.17
Date last produced	September 1954	September 1958	1959

THE MINERVA POSSIBILITY

The Belgian Minerva company made fine motor-cars from 1903. Early exponents of the Knight sleeve-valve engine, their beautifully-built touring cars remain highly regarded, and appealed to much the same inter-war market sector as was inhabited by Armstrong Siddeley.

The old firm was absorbed into the Belgian IFA-Excelsior group in 1935, but the name continued under new owner Matthieu Van Roggen. Its swansong was however the extraordinary TAM-18 model of 1937, powered by a transversely-mounted Ford V8 engine driving its front wheels. A handful of such cars were built before war intervened.

At war's end Van Roggen built small commercial vehicles, and acquired one of the prototypes designed by Professor Antonio Fessia for the Italian Caproni aircraft company, intending to franchise its construction. From unknown sources he acquired and fitted a side-valve horizontally opposed four-cylinder engine, and displayed the handsome cabriolet with Minerva badging on the European Show circuit in 1950, after which it vanished.

He negotiated manufacturing rights for Land Rover vehicles, and from 1950 supplied large numbers badged as Land Rover-Minervas to the Belgian military. He also negotiated a licence agreement for construction of the Sapphire with Armstrong Siddeley Motors Ltd, and built up 49 six-light saloons from CKD kits. One of these he converted to a four-door cabriolet.

To introduce the new Minerva product to the market, Van Roggen engaged high-profile motoring journalist and race driver Paul Frère, to drive a Sapphire overland from Brussels to Bombay. A second car was piloted by a cinematographer and his wife, who filmed this epic journey. Frère was required to write a book about the trek and was promised that the Sapphire would become his at its completion.

Frère's book, *La Croisière Minerva sur la route des Indes – Bruxelles-Bombay en automobile* (The Minerva Cruise on the road to India – Brussels to Bombay by car), tells in a matter-of-fact style the story of two Sapphires and two Land Rover-Minervas which drove from Belgium via France, Germany, Jugoslavia, Bulgaria, Turkey, Greece, Syria, Israel, Iraq, Iran and Afghanistan to India. Of the two Sapphires, that driven by Frère was fitted with the optional twin Stromberg carburettors, while the second was the standard car with single carb. Both were fitted with synchromesh transmissions, and were standard except for the carriage of a second spare wheel (not used in either case) and jerry cans for extra fuel. The Land Rover-Minervas were similarly standard issue.

The trip was a curious mix of international travelogue, motor vehicle testing regimen and a touch of the galloping gourmet. Frère describes in great detail his disgust at the Serbian hotel in which the teams were berthed, declaring that he would not bathe in a communally used zinc bath. Who could blame him? He describes their long wait for two sticks of bread and some coffee, while the locals quaffed slivovitz. He felt that the two other teams – who had gone ahead hoping to find something better – were probably fortunate to have slept in their cars.

Their trip appears to have been largely untroubled, except when Frère drove over an 'unexpected hump' at some 80mph and became airborne. The car landed heavily and deranged the front suspension, which remarkably was repaired by a blacksmith equipped with a welding kit in an Iranian village.

Their route covered many of the now-popular tourist sites including the rock-hewn necropolis of Petra, Darius's Castle at Persepolis and the Tomb of d'Akhara at Agra, with all the colour of snake-charmers, monster Baobab trees and the ruins of ancient fortresses thrown in for local colour.

The team was right royally received in the Middle East, enjoyed their introduction to the then-Shah of Iran, and viewed his collection of magnificent cars.

But their highest praise appears to have been reserved for the banquet laid on by Sheikh Hassan of Souhail in Baghdad, the centrepiece of which was an entire barbecued sheep.

Since Frère's car was required for display on the Minerva stand at the Brussels Motor Show early in 1954, he left the others in New Delhi to drive through the night to Bombay, where car and team boarded a ship bound for Belgium. On their return to Brussels, the car was dismantled for inspection, Van Roggen declared that he had lost interest in motor-car manufacture, the Sapphire was never displayed at the Motor Show, and Frère never received his car.

Minerva continued to build commercial vehicles until 1957, when the doors closed forever.

THE SAPPHIRE 234/236

1955-1958

Consistent with the company's tradition of offering vehicles in more than one market sector, and accepting that the Sapphire had moved upmarket both in terms of price and clientele, Armstrong Siddeley in 1955 introduced two versions of its smaller 2.3 litre cars – the Sapphire 236 and 234. Utilising a shared form, they covered two market segments with essentially similar cars – those seeking refined touring cars as successors to the 18hp, and a new market prioritising sporting performance and handling. While a prototype was circulating in June, 1954, the appearance of both models at the Earls Court Motor Show on 19th October, 1955 took most by surprise. Although both shared exterior bodywork and chassis, they were defined by their engines.

The Autocar said, in their issue of 28th October, 1955 that: "Whereas the 236 is more in keeping with earlier Armstrong Siddeley tradition, providing quiet, willing, easy-to-drive transportation, with more than average comfort for the passengers, the 234, which, body-wise, is externally and internally the same as the 236, has a great deal of extra punch from its four-cylinder engine, and thus will appeal especially to the performance enthusiast".

Work by the 1947-49 W O Bentley consultancy was again evident. The frame was a heavily braced dual rail design not unlike the Sapphire (which at this time became the Mark II Sapphire 346), carrying a front sub-frame welded rather than detachable, with independent front suspension by coils and wishbones, and semi-elliptics at the rear. Girling telescopic dampers were fitted all-round (enclosed within the coils at the front, angled onto the frame in the Alfa Romeo manner at the rear), although heavy-duty Armstrong dampers could be specified. As with the larger car, there were anti-roll bars fitted front and rear, and Telaflo adjustable rear dampers were available to special order.

Braking on both versions imitated the system of front trailing shoes and a Clayton Dewandre (later Girling) vacuum booster used on the 346, while steering was by variable ratio Burman recirculating ball mechanism. Steel 15-inch wheels shod with 6.40 X 15 cross-ply tyres were offered as standard wear, but centre-lock wire wheels painted silver or in body colour, or chromium plated, were optionally available. The last cars could be specified with Michelin or Pirelli radial ply tyres.

The six-cylinder 236 was a highly refined tourer in the tradition of the 16/18hp cars, offering ten more horsepower than the Whitley, and a taller final drive ratio. Its engine was substantially modified from the 18hp it replaced, but retained that car's silky performance. With internal changes to cylinder head and valves, the car was tested at 88mph (*Modern Motor*, July, 1957), bettering the factory's claim of 85mph, and returned 25mpg.

The British-made Manumatic transmission replaced the conventional clutch with one operated electrically from a micro-switch in the gearlever. One need only touch the lever to disengage the clutch, and a centrifugal mechanism supplied the take-up. Clutchless manual gearchanges were then available on Mercedes Benz (Hydrak), Renault (Ferlec), Fiat and Lancia (Saxomat) and others, employing hydraulic or pneumatic rams to operate conventional clutches by electric control. These systems were effective when in good condition, but their complicated maintenance defeated many repairmen, and they rapidly fell from market favour.

On the 236, the Manumatic system controlled an excellent all-synchromesh four-speed gearbox built in-house by Armstrong Siddeley, with the optional Laycock de Normanville electric overdrive available only on top gear. Later in its production life the 236 was offered with a conventional clutch, with or without overdrive. While never catalogued, one car was built with a preselector gearbox identical to the last 18hp, but although a preselectric version was listed for the 234, probably none was built. Sales of the 236 were always patchy, and production was discontinued in June, 1957 after 601 cars had been delivered.

If the 236 was refined, the 234 was raunchy, and broke new market ground for the company. Its four-cylinder engine was effectively two thirds of a Sapphire 346 engine, sharing the larger car's 90mm square bore and stroke, and its fundamental design. Many of its departures from the 346 specification – chiefly with respect to valves, pistons, compression ratio and crankshaft bearings – anticipated changes later incorporated in the Star Sapphire. It shared the four-speed synchromesh gearbox of the 236, but always with a conventional plate clutch, which the handbook warned "should not be disengaged at

speeds in excess of 5250rpm when changing gear unless the special competition clutch is fitted". Overdrive, when specified, operated on both third and fourth gears, giving six effective forward ratios.

The 234's engine produced 120bhp at 5000rpm fitted with twin inclined SU HD6 carburettors, thereby achieving the output targeted for the Bentley consultancy's 2322cc engine, but at a price. *The Autocar* in its road test of 5th October, 1956 commented: "...there is a certain amount of harshness which can be felt from a tick-over upwards through the speed range, accompanied by a noise-level more appropriate to the purely sports saloon... the 234 performs well, reaching 80mph quickly, even if not very quietly". Disregarding the engine's relative roughness, it outperformed many British rag-tops, reaching 25, 41 and 62mph on the indirects, ran on to 81mph in overdrive third, and in

favourable conditions topped the magic hundred in overdrive top.

However advanced and technically competent both the 236 and the 234 may have been, their body design produced mixed reactions. At its Motor Show debut, the Directors observed a muted public response to their new model, while Jaguar's 2.4 litre car was mobbed. In its 1956 road test of the 234, *The Autocar* said: "There is some conflict between the engine design and details of the chassis and coachwork". It is curious that the in-house design of the Sapphire – at once modern but faithful to its classical roots – was harmonious and instantly appealing, yet the 236/234 used multiple styling cues which fought each other rather than forming a unified whole.

The Sapphire-like radiator grille stamped the new cars as Armstrong Siddeleys, but there the attachment to any other model faded. The coachwork seemed designed by a committee, its outcome a majority decision rather than unanimity. Even its interior trim contrasted beautifully-finished walnut facia and door-cappings with vinyl trim material, although leather remained a special option. Some point to the apocryphal tale of a company Director insisting the roof-line be raised to allow him to wear his Homburg while seated in the rear, while others excuse the design as being 'ahead of its time'.

In practical terms, the body was light and spacious, with Hiduminium 22 alloy used for body panels other than turret and wings, which were fabricated from lightweight steel. With all-forward hinged slender doors opening at right-angles, interior space was greater than on the larger 346 (whose vast front doors extended the front wing line while occupying passenger space). Multiple curves and minimal extrusions made it quiet through the air even at high speeds, and contemporary reports noted it was taut and rattle-free.

Compared to its major competitor – the Jaguar 2.4 litre – the 236/234 was something of an anachronism. The Jaguar was that company's first exercise in monocoque construction. Its engine was an understressed, oversquare six which probably gave more dependable service than its larger undersquare brethren. Its body design, although described by one observer as 'tubby', had a unity which was ultimately refined into the Mark 2 and S series, sharing the 236/234 cars' silence and integrity at speed.

While the market had no doubts about the Jaguar, and bought it enthusiastically, it was unsure about the 236/234. Demand for the 234 was never strong, but quickened once news spread of its 'sleeper' status as a performance saloon. But Armstrong Siddeley's decision to build a four-cylinder performance car fell foul of a market which accorded status to a six over a four, regardless of the four's excellence.

The refinement of the 236 was possibly overshadowed by its price relative to other competent and refined touring cars then available – from British manufacturers and elsewhere – and its odd coachwork.

Conflicting priorities at Parkside meant that pressures for military equipment denied the smaller Sapphire its own permanent production line, instead sharing the 346 facility as and when it could. Since tales persist of dealers who never received cars they ordered, we may

conclude that the Directors were not committed to their new model, preferring to give priority to the popular 346 and assured markets for their aeronautical products. Only 1406 'baby Sapphires' were built between April, 1955 and October, 1958. Three cars departed from the standard coachwork; one was remodelled as a utility by the Experimental Department, who constructed a cabriolet on another chassis, while Italian coachbuilder Michelotti produced a handsome four-door saloon for a Spanish client.

In his book *Armstrong Siddeley Motors*, Bill Smith tells that, during the gestation of the small Sapphires, the company flirted with the notion of building DKW cars under licence. The DKW was beautifully built in the German manner, but was at best a self-willed design. Powered by a three-cylinder two-stroke engine with a propensity for belching smoke and stalling in traffic when its fuel-oil mixture was not quite right, it was not cheap to build. Perhaps we should conclude that muddled thinking prevailed at Parkside at the time, and leave it at that.

Armstrong Siddeley present two new 2·3 litre *Sapphires* to join the famous *Sapphire 346*

Sapphire 236
with the amazing MANUMATIC no-clutch pedal gear change.

Armstrong Siddeley have set a high standard of refinement in their new 2·3 litre 6 cylinder saloon. There is no clutch pedal. You simply move a centrally placed gear lever straight into the gear you want at the precise moment you want it—and you're in! No snatch. No clashing of gears. Just a continuous smooth flow of power. It is a great thrill to make perfect changes easily and quickly with this new type of control.

You get unmatched smooth performance at all speeds up to 85 m.p.h. Yet you will average 30 m.p.g. on the open road. The Sapphire 236 costs £1104 (plus £461 P.T.).

Sapphire 234
OVER 100 M.P.H.
Synchromesh gearbox and central gear lever.

The new Sapphire 2.3 litre 120 b.h.p. 4 cylinder saloon is a car that allies exceptional performance to the greatest possible refinement in styling and finish. Using the 4-speed synchromesh gearbox you can accelerate from 0 to 60 m.p.h. in 12.8 secs. and in top there is over 100 m.p.h. at your command.

Wonderfully responsive. Superbly safe, with its large size vacuum servo assisted brakes, it will give you immense pleasure to drive under all possible road and traffic conditions. The Sapphire 234 costs £1065 (plus £445 P.T.).

BOTH the Sapphire 236 and 234 are identical in exterior appearance, refinement and luxury. Both are full 5-seater saloons with 131 cu. ft. luggage boots. Both come straight from the drawing boards, workshops and testing grounds that produce the brilliantly successful Sapphire 346 and the world famous Sapphire jet which powers many of the world's fastest aircraft.

Both have NYLON FINISHED UPHOLSTERY, very durable and easy to clean.

Outstanding features include: double bulkhead for super silence, extra wide bucket seats in front; full four-point visibility from the driver's seat, and quick-lift front offside window; air conditioner unit; instrument dials have ultra-violet lighting; windscreen washers; right-angle opening doors with concealed forward hinges for safety; non-corrosive body; luxury walnut instrument panel. An overdrive can be fitted as an optional extra on both cars. Wire wheels can be fitted as an optional extra on the Sapphire 234.

There is a choice of seven exceptionally attractive body colours in plain and two-tone versions.

Drive whichever model you prefer, you will be more than impressed

Write to **ARMSTRONG SIDDELEY MOTORS LTD., COVENTRY,** *for cat. No. 236, or No. 234.*

 MEMBER OF THE HAWKER SIDDELEY GROUP

Above: The production 236, outwardly identical to its 234 sibling, and beautifully finished if visually unusual.

Left: Dating from October 19, 1955, this advertisement in *The Motor* packs a very large amount of information onto the page about the two new, smaller Sapphires. The rendering is repeated on the sales brochures for the cars, the work of noted artist Terence Cuneo. His trademark running mouse is however absent, or has been expunged.

Above: Another Cuneo illustration, this time showing the compact interior of the 236/234, but a realistically proportioned occupant (for a change).

Top left: The 236/234 four speed manual transmission was built in-house by Armstrong Siddeley. This example shows the optional Laycock de Normanville electric overdrive, which in the 236 operated only on top gear, but on the 234 provided six effective ratios when engaged on third and fourth.

Left: Rear suspension of the 236/234 employed telescopic dampers attached to the frame at an angle to the vertical, contributing to the model's noted stability.

Common to both versions was limited luggage accommodation, due to the severely sloping boot-lid.
Madam appears suitably apprehensive.

The visually similar 234, here shown with the optional chromed centre-lock wire wheels.

Above: Armstrong Siddeley operated their private testing ground – the first British motor manufacturer to do so – at Anstey, between Leicester and Coventry. Here a 236/234 runs through the water splash. After the opening of Anstey, every Armstrong Siddeley car was driven around the test facility before being cleared for delivery.

Right: Sporting cockpit. Note the large tachometer in the centre of the instrument panel, and the overdrive switch to the right of the steering column.

Views of the only 234 bodied by an outside coachbuilder, Michelotti of Italy. It was constructed to the order of a client in Madrid, Spain. These Armstrong Siddeley Motors photographs date from May 1958. The car's fate is unknown.

Factory designation	Sapphire 234	Sapphire 236
Date introduced	April 1956	October 1956
Motor type	4 cyl 4-stroke in-line water-cooled ohv	6-cyl 4-stroke in-line water-cooled ohv
Dimensions	90 X 90mm = 2290cc	70 X 100mm = 2309cc
Power/rpm	120bhp @ 5000rpm	85bhp @ 4400rpm
Fuel feed	mech pump from rear to 2 X SU carbs	same but single Stromberg carb
Ignition	battery and coil	same
Transmission type	4-spd + elec o'drive centre floor change	4-spd initially, later + optional o'drive
Ratios	15.692 9.703 6.450 (5.108) 4.545 (3.536) Rev 13.55	same (note overdrive not available on 3rd when specified for the 236)
	(note overdrive ratios for 3rd and 4th in brackets)	
Final drive ratio	Salisbury 3HA (later 7HA) 4.545:1	same
Clutch	Borg & Beck hydraulic	Manumatic electric clutch, later Borg & Beck hydraulic also available
Steering	Burman F recirculating ball, variable ratio	same
Suspension		
Front	independent by coils & trailing wishbones	same
Rear	semi-elliptic springs, anti-roll bars front & rear	same
	telescopic dampers all round	same
Brakes	Girling 11" (front) 2 lead shoes (rear) 1 lead/1 trail	same
	Girling vacuum servo	same
Wheels	15" Dunlop steel disc. Painted or chromed wires opt	same
Tyres	6.40 X 15" cross ply, 175 X 15" radials later optional	same
Dimensions		
Wheelbase	9'3"	same
Track front	4'7½"	same
Track rear	4'6 5/16"	same
Overall length	15'	same
Overall width	5'8½"	same
Height	5'1¾"	same
Unladen weight	27 cwt (factory figure, some sources say lighter)	same
Factory coachwork	4-dr 4-lt saloon	same
Variants	1 coachbuilt by Michelotti, 1 cabrio	nil
Performance		
Max speed (mph)	97 (Autocar road test 5.10.1956)	88 (Modern Motor road test July 1957)
Fuel consumption (mpg)	22-27	25 (on test. Factory claimed 30mpg)
Number produced	806	601
Prices	£1510 incl Purchase Tax	£1565 incl PT
Date last produced	October 1958	December 1957

STAR SAPPHIRE – GLORIOUS SWANSONG
1958-1960

The British motor industry in the late 1950s was at the crossroads. Some Austin, Morris and Wolseley models relied on engines designed in the 1930s, Riley was in its death throes as a badge-engineered Wolseley, AC still used the ohc 2-litre engine designed in 1921, while even the future of Rolls-Royce was openly questioned.

Some British makers' outmoded designs competed with fresh new models from Europe, yet Armstrong Siddeley contrived to be the first company to produce a new car after war's end. The 16/18hp series was followed by the stunning new 3.4 litre Sapphire, and two more new cars – the 236/234. That competence largely derived from their involvement in aircraft manufacture.

The Star Sapphire was introduced in October, 1958, and was such a radically new car that it warrants its own model chapter. *Motor Sport* described it as: "A Gentleman's Carriage which is Extremely Easy to Drive Yet Exceeds 100mph, with the Security of Girling Disc Brakes". *Top Gear* said in 1959: "Effortless running is a feature of the car, but although the major controls including the gearchange system are all 'power-assisted', the Sapphire will please the keen driver. It would be wrong to imagine that this car cannot be handled in an enterprising

manner. From the driver's point of view... it can be driven hard without effort, and it is a safe machine to handle at speed on the open road". The company's own promotions styled the Star Sapphire 'The Managing Director's Car' a decade before Triumph's MD-series 2000, declaring "The new Star Sapphire is tailor-made for the man at the top: the man who demands absolute efficiency, sparkling performance and club chair comfort". The *Autosport* test of 26th June, 1959 quoted its maximum speed as 105mph, and a 0-60mph time of 12.9 seconds, placing its performance amongst the faster British sports cars.

Visually very similar to its predecessor, the only panels common to the 346 Sapphire were its boot-lid, scuttle, rear wheel-arches and inner front mudguards. Colour ranges included some finishes used on Rolls-Royce and Bentley cars, perhaps most notably the attractive sand-over-sable combination. Its front-hinged front doors, concealed door-hinges, radiator grille, bonnet line, chrome waist strip and tail-lamps were all new, as was its interior. There, luxurious Vaumol leathers on split bench front seats and shaped rears were available in single or contrasting colours, burled walnut was used for facia and door-trims, and hood-lining was available in either the Sapphire's off-white PVC material, or woollen cloth. A new heating system provided separate supply to the rear compartment, including rear window demisting. Later cars were fitted with 7-inch Lucas PL headlamps.

The luggage compartment was fully carpeted, as were all interior floors. Optional equipment included radio, rear picnic tables, Webasto fabric sunroof, laminated windscreen, lockable glovebox lid, fast-action front window lifts, radiator blind, fitted luggage, wing mirrors, dipping interior mirror and a flagstaff. Extended rails for the front seats were available to order, and some were fitted with Reutter reclining mechanisms. Refrigerated airconditioning was also (but rarely) fitted upon request, at which time the engine was mounted on rubber at four points to allow space for the necessary hardware.

Beneath the surface were more than cosmetic changes. The engine was bored to 97mm but retained the 346 Sapphire's 90mm stroke for a capacity of 3990cc. Power lifted to 165bhp but at the lower engine speed of 4250rpm, and mid-range torque was significantly improved. There was a new block, cylinder head, crankshaft, camshaft, connecting rods, pistons, valves, bearings, flywheel, sump, valve cover, inlet manifold, air-cleaners and hydraulically-tensioned timing chain. Dual carburettors were standard equipment, initially Stromberg DIV42 but later Zenith WIA42, the latter giving worthwhile savings in fuel consumption. For late series cars modified water-jacketing in the block, and a larger capacity sump, were designed to enhance cooling capacity.

Only one transmission was offered – the Borg Warner DG-series 3-speed automatic. It was provided with a variable speed second gear hold, by which the driver could adjust the change into top from 15 to 65mph by a vertical slide on the facia. Although fitted with a torque-converter, the gearbox contained a direct drive clutch which locked when in top gear. Final drive ratio was 3.77:1 via a Salisbury differential, and wheels were 16-inch Dunlop discs similar to the later 346 Sapphire.

For the first time an Armstrong Siddeley used 12-inch Girling disc brakes on the front wheels, while 12-inch finned drums used one leading and one trailing shoe each on the back. The discs were operated by double-piston callipers, assisted by a Girling vacuum booster and reservoir.

Emphasising the company's priority on quality coachwork, the award at the 1958 Earl's Court Motor Show – at which the Star Sapphire was first exhibited – of a Gold Medal for coachwork on vehicles priced below £4000 was the subject of this prominent advertisement in *The Autocar* of 7th November, 1958.

237

Opposite page: The prototype Star Sapphire, seen here, was a Mark II Sapphire 346 onto which had been grafted the features of the new model. This car survives.

The chassis itself was strengthened, especially its front cross-member, and progressively deformable bump stops augmented the rear semi-elliptics and the Girling or Armstrong dampers for a better-controlled ride. Steering on all cars was power-assisted, but omitted the variable assistance offered on the late 346 cars.

The 346 limousine continued in production until January 1960, when the Star version arrived, looked familiar, but differed markedly from its predecessor. Engines were similar to those of the Star saloon, but were all mounted at four points to the frame, allowing space for airconditioning equipment when specified for £514 extra. In standard guise there was a single Zenith WIA42 carburettor, giving 140bhp, and developing maximum torque at just 1750rpm. Twin carbs for a similar output to the saloon were optionally available, as was an electrically-operated glass division replacing the standard sliding partition.

The standard limousine transmission was the Humber-sourced all-synchromesh four-speed unit fitted to the 346 Sapphire, although the Borg Warner automatic was an extra-cost option. Sadly the preselectric gearbox of the 346 was never available. Final drive was 4.09:1 like the Sapphire saloon, but large 7.60 X 15 tyres helped restore overall gearing which approximated that of the saloon.

Seats in the front compartment were shaped for extra comfort, and trim design was markedly different to that in the preceding model; leather was offered either throughout or to the front compartment only, with West-of-England cloth to the rear. As before rear passengers had their own heater and radio, to which were added airconditioning controls and the division-lowering switch when fitted.

The major external changes were an enlarged boot-lid which allowed extra stowage space, the Star style radiator grille, smaller 15-inch wheels, new bumpers and different tail-lamps incorporating amber flasher lenses. Like the late saloons, the limousines used Lucas PL headlamps.

As a stop-gap model between the Star and its proposed replacement, one Mark 2 Star saloon prototype was built, attempting to modernise the production car by fitting quad headlamps, a wider rear window, revised interior trim, 15-inch wheels and the limousine boot-lid.

Both the Star saloon and limousine were beautifully built, graceful, swift and comfortable cars, which were very competitively priced. Yet by 1960 then-owners Bristol Siddeley Engines Ltd suffered a loss of £70 on every car sold, when its contracts to build Sunbeam Alpine roadsters for Rootes, and aero engines for domestic and military consumption, were highly profitable.

With the help of 20/20 hindsight, one wonders if the Star and its limousine were not substantially underpriced, since at an ex-Works price of £1763 for the saloon, and £2222 for the limousine, they left most if not all their competitors gasping. What were regarded as luxury saloons like the automatic Rover 3-litre (ponderous and comparatively under-equipped at £1704), Daimler Majestic (£2495) and Bentley S2 (£4195) could not equal the Star's mix of speed, handling, build quality and passenger comfort. Another pretender to the 'luxury' tag, the 3-litre Wolseley 6/99, sold for £885 but was an unworthy suitor.

The Star limousine offered even better value when compared to the Rolls-Royce Phantom V at almost treble the price (£6600), and the dreary Daimler DK400 (£4191).

Yet in its only full year of production (1959), just 567 Star saloons were delivered, and only 77 limousines were built in total. The 234 had already been discontinued, and plans for a new range of cars were denied development funding in 1957 and again in 1959. The costs of re-tooling for a planned new car in 1962 were estimated at £1.25million, but with both Armstrong Siddeley and Bristol cars haemorrhaging money, the Board of Bristol Siddeley Engines resolved on 19th January, 1960 to abandon car production, sell off the Bristol manufacturing operation and terminate Armstrong Siddeley from July 31, 1960.

Rather than lament the passing of the marque, perhaps we should be glad that the bean-counters were not allowed to besmirch the Armstrong Siddeley name. There is no doubt that the very last cars were every bit as good as the finest of their predecessors, and adhered strongly to the production ethos of the company's founder.

Brochure image leaving no doubt about the Star Sapphire's intended market.

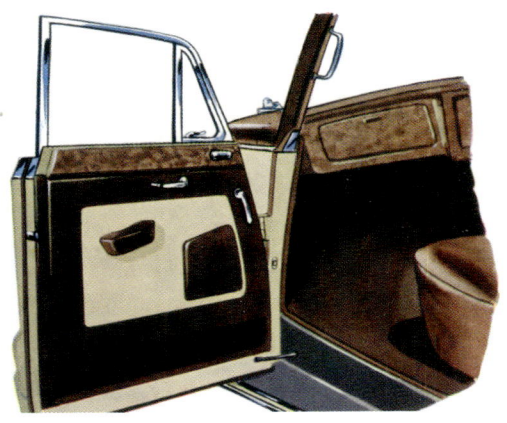

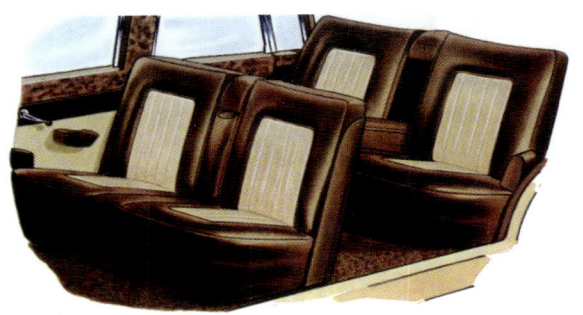

Top left: The Star's impressive cockpit featured burl walnut panelling for dashboard and door-cappings. Note the unobstructed floor area. The vertical slide to the left of the instruments varied the speed at which the automatic gearbox changed from second into top gear.

Centre left: Unlike its predecessor, the Star's front doors were front-hinged, and used concealed rather than exposed hinges. As before, there were cubby boxes in the very wide door cavities.

Left: Replacing the 346 Sapphire's front and rear benches were effectively four separate armchairs. The driver's seat was separately adjusted from that of the front seat passenger, and heated air was delivered from outlets beneath the rear cushion. Leather could be supplied in single colours or in duo tones, as here.

Above: The luggage compartment was similar to the 346 Sapphire in size and shape, but was always fully carpeted.

The graceful forms of the production Star Sapphire, the company still visually attaching its products to aircraft.

The Star Sapphire long wheelbase limousine was introduced early in 1960. This car was fitted with optional refrigerated airconditioning, identified by the two extra intake grilles abreast of the radiator grille.

Above: As always the limousine was sumptuously equipped for rear seat passengers. Annoyingly this brochure photo is retouched from an earlier image of the 346 limousine, so does not show the Star's different trim patterns on doors and side-panels.

Above right: The standard Star Sapphire limousine, without airconditioning grilles, was a handsome machine.

Opposite page: The Star limousine used a much-enlarged boot-lid, as clearly shown in this image from the 1959 Earls Court Motor Show, where this prototype was exhibited.

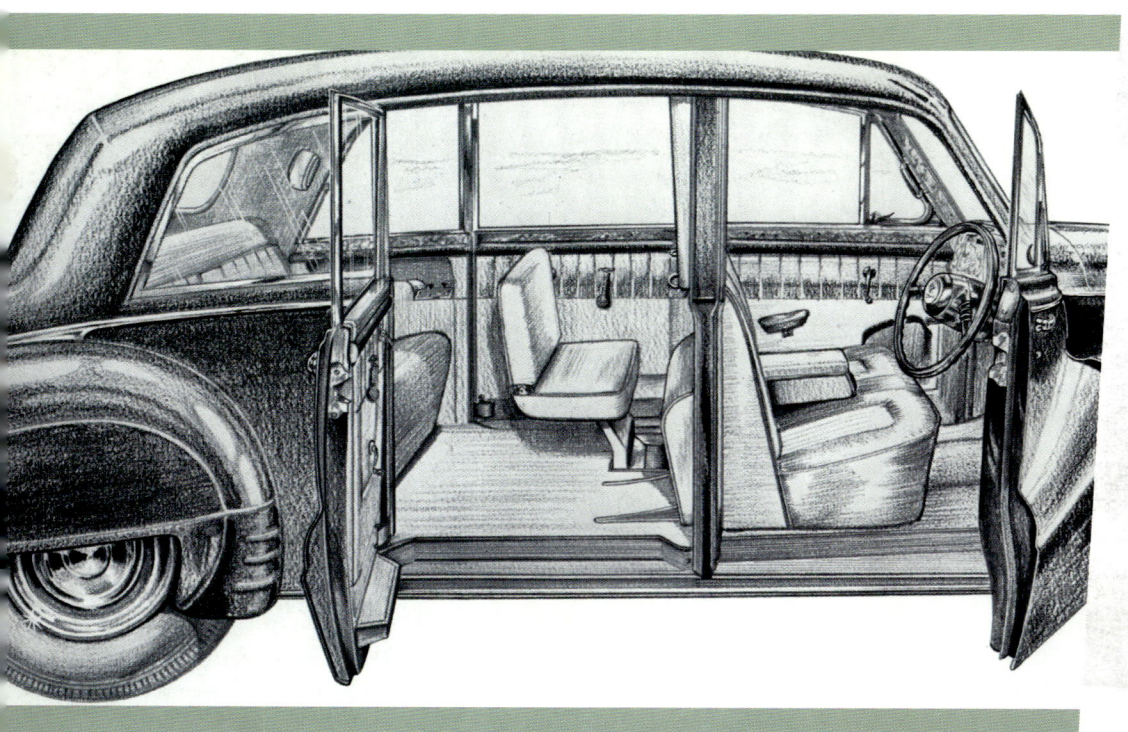

Perfection for seven

Above: This brochure image shows the part-vertical pleating which was a feature of the Star limousine's interior trim. Note also the semi-individual seats for chauffeur and footman.

Right: One of the very last advertisements for the Armstrong Siddeley marque, dated May 11, 1960, and published in *The Motor*. Car production ended on July 31st.

It's the new Armstrong Siddeley Star Sapphire Limousine

Mechanically, it's the same flawless piece of automobile engineering that has brought tributes from technical correspondents everywhere. But the limousine body has been splendidly re-styled; it's longer, lower and even better appointed than before. There's a larger rear compartment with wider, deeper seats; and altogether seven people can travel in ambassadorial comfort. And there's more luggage space, too.

Power steering and disc brakes, of course, and a synchromesh gearbox is standard and the automatic gearbox optional. Another excellent option is full air conditioning, which provides the extra blessing of positive refrigeration as well as heating control. That means you're completely independent of the weather.

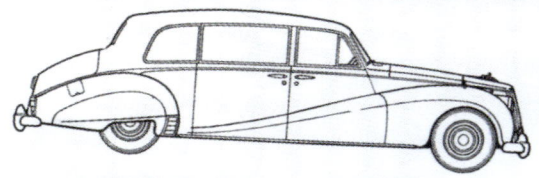

This Star Sapphire Limousine is a luxury car that has been styled for comfort to the nth degree. The wonder is that such prodigal comfort can be coupled to such refreshing performance, and at a price of only £3,149 (inc PT).

THE NEW STAR SAPPHIRE LIMOUSINE

ARMSTRONG SIDDELEY MANUFACTURED BY A DIVISION OF BRISTOL SIDDELEY

Factory designation	Star Sapphire	Star Sapphire limousine
Date introduced	Earls Court Motor Show, October 1958	January 1960
Motor type	6-cyl 4-stroke in-line water-cooled ohv	same
Dimensions	97 X 90mm = 3990cc	same
Power/rpm	165bhp @ 4250rpm	140bhp @ 4250rpm
Fuel feed	mech pump from rear tank to 2 Strombergs or Zeniths	same but single Zenith carb
Ignition	battery & coil	
Transmission type	Borg Warner DG 3-spd & rev automatic	4-spd & rev synchromesh (BW automatic optional)
Ratios	8.64-17.575 5.41-10.82 3.77:1 Rev 7.574-15.148	(synchro) 12.8 8.55 5.81 4.091:1 Rev 13.54:1
	variable intermediate gear hold	(auto) 9.44-20.3 5.87-12.62 4.091:1 Rev 8.22-17.67:1
Final drive ratio	3.77:1 hypoid bevel	4.091:1 for both transmissions
Clutch	torque converter	(synchro) Borg & Beck 10" single dry plate
Steering	Burman power-assisted recirculating ball	same
Suspension		
Front	independent by coils & wishbones, anti-roll bar	same
Rear	semi-elliptic springs, Girling or Armstrong dampers	same
Brakes	Girling 12" disc brakes at front, 12" drums rear	same front, 11" drums rear
Wheels	Dunlop steel disc wheels, 16" diameter	same but 15" diameter
Tyres	6.70 X 16" cross ply, options incl Michelin radials	7 60 X 15" cross ply
Dimensions		
Wheelbase	9'6"	11'3"
Track front	4'9 7/8"	4'10 7/8"
Track rear	4'9½"	5'1"
Overall length	16'2"	17'9"
Overall width	6'2"	6'2½"
Height	5'2"	5'7"
Unladen weight	35½ cwt	37 cwt
Factory coachwork	6-light 4-door saloon	6-light 4-door 7-seat limousine
Variants	1 prototype Mark II version, 1960	airconditioned version with detail body modifications
Performance		
Max speed (mph)	105 (Autsport road test 26.6.1959)	not known
Fuel consumption (mpg)	17	
Number produced	903	77 (incl 2 prototypes & 1 chassis)
Prices	£2498.14.2 incl Purchase Tax	(synchro) £3149.13.4 incl PT (auto) £3314.14.2 (aircond) + £513.10.10
Date last produced	July 1960	May 1960

ARMSTRONG
SIDDELEY

You cannot buy a better car

BIBLIOGRAPHY

Title	Author	Publisher/Date	ISBN
Advertising Armstrong Siddeley 1904-1960	Bill Smith & Daniel Young	Yesteryear Books, 1996	ISBN 873078196
Armstrong Siddeley	John Wright	Marque Classic Series, 2005	ISBN0947079904
Armstrong Siddeley – An Auto Review Book	Rod Ward	Zeteo Publishing	ISBN9781900482533
Armstrong Siddeley 1920-1960	Ed Colin Pitt	Unique Motor Books	
Armstrong Siddeley Cars 1945-1960	Ed R M Clarke	Brooklands Books	
Armstrong Siddeley Collection 1927-1930	Ed R M Clarke	Brooklands Books	
Armstrong Siddeley Collection 1931-1932	Ed R M Clarke	Brooklands Books	
Armstrong Siddeley Collection 1933-1934	Ed R M Clarke	Brooklands Books	
Armstrong Siddeley Collection 1935-1936	Ed R M Clarke	Brooklands Books	
Armstrong Siddeley Motors	Bill Smith	Veloce, 2006	ISBN190478836-X
Armstrong Siddeley – The Original 346 Sapphire	R P Bradly	Limula Pty Ltd, E North	ISBN9780980426922
Armstrong Siddeley – The Parkside Story 1896-1939	Ray Cook	RRHT No 11, 1988	ISBN0951171038
Armstrong Siddeley – The Postwar Cars	R P Bradly	MRP, 1989	ISBN0947981276
Australian Dictionary of Motoring, The	Pedr Davis	Bookworks Pty Ltd, 2001	ISBN1876953004
A-Z of British Coachbuilders – 1919-1960	Nick Walker	Bay View Books, 1997	ISBN1870979931
Beaulieu Encyclopaedia of the Automobile Vols 1 & 2	Ed Nick Georgano	The Stationery Office, 2000	ISBN0117023191
Beaulieu Encyclopaedia of the Automobile Coachbuilding	Ed Nick Georgano	The Stationery Office, 2001	ISBN0117027502
Cars of the Thirties and Forties	Michael Sedgwick	Rigby, 1979	ISBN0727007238
Complete Catalogue of British Cars, The	D Culshaw & P Horrobin	Macmillan, 1974	
Evening and the Morning, The	Ed Bernard Coaling	Toon & Heath Ltd, 1956	
La Croisière MINERVA sur la route des Indes	Paul Frère	Editions JaRie, 1954	
Parkside- Armstrong Siddeley to Rolls-Royce	Roy Lawton	RRHT No 39, 2008	ISBN9781872922355
Pre-War Armstrong Siddeley	Trevor Alder	TSB229, 1995	
Silence of the Sphinx, The	Ronald A R Kerkhoven	Museuon Den Haag, 1995	ISBN9068251678
Stoneleigh Motors – an Armstrong Siddeley Company	Alan Betts	RRHT No 37, 2006	ISBN1872922341
Ultimate Armstrong Siddeley	Ed Colin Pitt	Unique Motor Books	ISBN1841554081
Walter Wilson: Portrait of an Inventor	A Gordon Wilson	Gerald Duckworth, 1986	ISBN0715621270
W O Bentley – Engineer	Donald Bastow	Haynes, 1978	ISBN0854292152

DVD INSTRUCTIONS

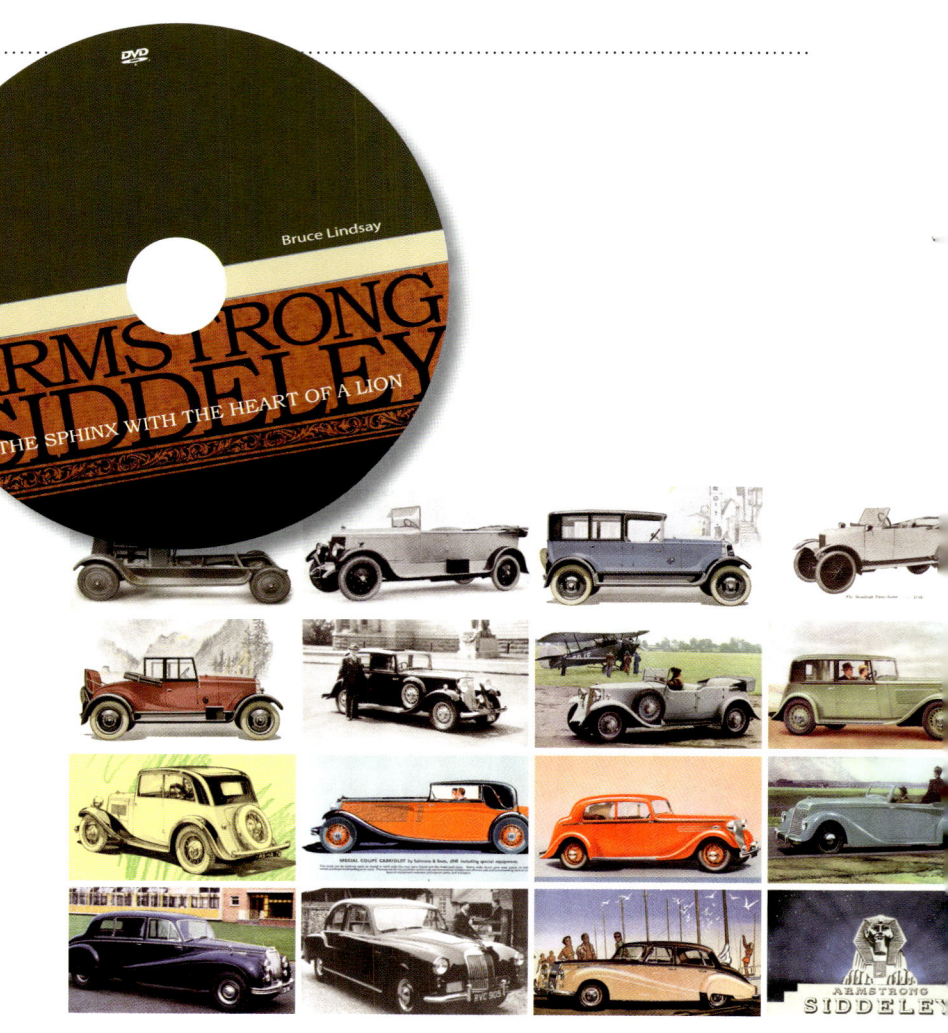

The DVD mounted on the back cover contains images of a representative sample of the very large number of promotional catalogues, produced by Armstrong Siddeley Motors Ltd and their dealers, between 1919 and 1960.

Your computer will require Acrobat Reader to open and view the contents, and you may download the latest version from www.adobe.com if it is not already installed.

If you operate a PC, the DVD contains automatic start-up software, which will allow you to view thumbnails of the contents. The brochures are arranged in chronological order, and when you click on any one of them, they will open to reveal all pages. They are accessible both by year and in groups relating to the book chapters.

If you operate a Mac, the automatic start-up function will not assist, but on opening you should go to index.html, and then to Introduction, and navigate your way through the brochures according to your choice.